Moving at th
How to Live the Dash

Patrick J. Oliver, Ph.D., D. Min.

Copyright © 2019 All rights reserved. This material is protected by the copyright laws of the United States of America. This material may not be copied or reprinted for commercial gain or profit. No part of this publication may be reproduced or transmitted in any form or by any means, electronic or mechanical, including photocopying, recording, or placing on the Internet, without written permission from the author.

ISBN: 9781096335061

DEDICATION

For D'Anthony Marcel Johnson, Sr.

I vividly recall the unquantifiable joy I experienced on May 10, 1992 (his sunrise) and the unbearable agony I felt on May 14, 2018 (his sunset). **Both dates are forever engrained in my heart, obviously evoking distinctly different emotional reactions. Our beloved D'Anthony Marcel was undoubtedly one of a kind, a force of nature!** But like all of us, he was an imperfect being. He was also an undeniably unique & powerful spirit that left an indelible mark on all his family and friends. He did not let the mistakes he made define him and because of this fortitude, the faith LaShonda and I had in him never waned. D'Anthony was determined to learn from the setbacks and disappointments and was enthusiastic about the future and what it had in store for him. He genuinely desired to right the wrongs of his life. **He was clearly on an introspective journey** and appeared to finally understand and accept all the words of guidance, expectation, and encouragement LaShonda and I had given him throughout the years of his life. I know in my heart that he finally "got it" and that sentiment was emotionally and passionately communicated to me at the hospital from the vocal cords of his younger brother Darrell Jr. During unquestionably the most difficult moment of my life—after the Surgeon and Chaplain had just relayed to us that D'Anthony had died—I so desperately needed to hear those words uttered from his little brother's mouth. Powerful words that I know God intended for me to hear at that time.

Those timely words provided the counsel and surgery my soul so desperately needed. I desperately needed to hear a soul-knitting melody after the sky had literally cracked and my soul was severely scarred hearing the doctor and chaplain utter words **no parent EVER wants to hear!** Darrell Jr. echoed the visionary and heartfelt words of his big brother to me. God then used them to deliver into me the necessary strength to stabilize my heart and steady my legs and feet.

Hopefulness and positive transformation were evident in D'Anthony's actions before his untimely passing as he had indeed begun to **Move at the**

Speed of Intention but more specifically, displayed the longing desire to be a present, loving and doting father to his own son. He was undeniably ready to **Live-his-Dash** and more fully demonstrate that he **came from GOOD STOCK!** As his dad, this has provided me a semblance of peace. It will continue to be a source of emotional strength and mental endurance as I face many tough days, months, and years ahead. I will forever cherish AND be grateful for the 26 years God blessed us with D'Anthony. His light will illuminate beamingly in my heart and throughout my entire being until the day God whispers my name. Yes, death may have ended our son's earthly existence, but it did not sever our relationship with him. The unconditional love his mom and I have for him is perpetual, so it will never cease to exist. We love him but **God loves him BEST**.

Our earthly lives can be abruptly ended or irrevocably changed in a heartbeat. As such, it's imperative that we **do not count the time** we have remaining but rather do all within our power to **make our remaining time count**. I pray as you read this book, you receive a blessing of hope, motivation, personal empowerment, and individual responsibility as I did when I was blessed with the opportunity to read it well before its release. You can decide on this day, where necessary, to **change the trajectory of your life** and BELIEVE that you can accomplish anything you set your mind to. As long as there is breath in your body, it's never too late to **Move at the Speed of Intention**. It's never too late for us to make our own mark on this world. We all have been blessed with opportunities to leave positive imprints on those we encounter and through our example, encourage and inspire them to pay it forward. **I pray that you permit this book to provoke and shake you to not just dwell in possibility**, but to instead **be intent on allowing your tomorrow to become your today**. Doing so will give power to the currency of today so that it may light your tomorrow.

While there is no playbook for recovering after unimaginable, heartbreaking, and traumatic loss or when experiencing extremely difficult situations in life, I find that giving the grief words can help permeate light in these darkest of circumstances. I can't properly express in words how emotionally moved I am that my little brother has dedicated this book to my son. However, I am not surprised because we were raised by our mom to always support, encourage, and uplift each other no matter the circumstances. Dr. P's penning of this work has certainly reinforced and validated that upbringing. And I am sure our mom is just as moved and proud as I am. Thank you,

Little Brother, for the intentional LOVE shared BY this book and IN this book. I am eternally grateful to you for this playbook for living and for using the life of your oldest nephew to weave a soul stirring and deeply personal narrative echoing the blessing and promise of intentional living. **May the e2I champion be ignited in all of us**. Today!

Rest Well in Eternity, My Eldest Prince!!!

In God's Hands, Darrell Anthony Johnson Sr.

TABLE OF CONTENTS

Acknowledgements	7
Introduction	11
Chapter 1: Eventuality vs. Intentionality	17
Chapter 2: Your Move	22
Chapter 3: Cancelled Reservations	29
Chapter 4: RSVP to God's Invitation	33
Chapter 5: Inhale Purpose. Exhale Destiny	40
Chapter 6: Living in the Key of Life: B Natural	45
Chapter 7: The Testimony of Tattoos	60
Chapter 8: Conversations with the Pregnant Graveyard	64
Chapter 9: Turn Tomorrow into Today	76
Chapter 10: LivINg the Dream	92
Chapter 11: Tolls on the Road to Intention	103
Chapter 12: e2I Tool Suite	108
Chapter 13: Epilogue	146
APPENDIX A. NOTES FROM THE PIANO BENCH.	162
APPENDIX B. e2I TRAITS.	164
APPENDIX C. EULOGY SERMON NOTES.	170

ACKNOWLEDGEMENTS

I wrote *Moving at the Speed of Intention* in 12 weeks in the midst of a myriad of whirlwind life events. However, the genesis of this book has been in construction for over 17 years. Key concepts have been matured since I began teaching them in Bible Study, preaching sermon series, and emphasizing their central themes in professional, familial, and communal spaces. The tragic death of my nephew D'Anthony in May 2018 brought this project to life. This crystalized manuscript is the homily I preached at his funeral. This book, like his funeral homily, is addressed to the living on matters of faith and emphasizes the role his life will continue to play in the lives of the living. Moving at the speed of intention had significant liftoff on the runway of his life when the balance of borrowed time unexpectedly came due. I want to acknowledge and thank God for His intentional love and creative genius. It is only by God's grace that you are holding this book in your hands. His power and presence have turned my mourning into dancing. The countless lives stung by my nephew's death have in a chorus demanded their lives be stained by the life-defining and life-altering principles heralded at his funeral and burial. Out of our own pain and suffering, our Wounded Healer, Christ, is bringing forth healing and transformation.

  I want to thank mother, Barbara Joyce, and grandmother, Betty Jean, for crafting and conditioning my capacity to marry vision and intention. Your love and encouragement have been bottomless treasures for me. Your tireless examples of purposeful action in the face of overwhelming odds would have made most people shrink. Instead, you, with undying faith in the living God, have faced and conquered giants. *"We are not where we are from... We live in the projects but are not from the projects... We come from good stock"* were soul food and clarion calls to our God-shaped identities. Your identities and affirmations provided fuel for our God-sized dreams to intentionally pursue and possess the 'other than' that existed.

  I want to thank my siblings Tim, Darrell, and Patricia for being my heroes. I didn't have to look far for i.d.o.l.s (**i**nspirational **d**isciples **o**f **l**iving **s**uccess) growing up. Your personal and vocational excellence has provided and continues to be an epicenter of continual inspiration to me. Your unparalleled love, intelligence, sense of humor, genius, determination, sensitivity, compassion, selflessness, and boldness quickens me to joyfully testify "my siblings are better than yours!" ☺ I am transformed by your passion and burden for intentional living. Darrell, your loss has been heaven's gain. Thank you for grieving and living out loud. The Lord's hands are not amputated in your struggle. Thank you for teaching us how to reimagine a future that does not divorce itself from a painful present. You are an All-Star father and PawPaw. Thank you for being an e2I Champion. Your lived experience has served as a ghostwriter for this book.

To my kings and inheritance, you two have taught me how to love love. Patrick II and Jireh, you inspire and ignite me to be a better Christian, a better man, and a better father, brother, friend, citizen, change agent, and steward of influence. I love loving you and being loved by you. Save Jesus Christ, you are the best and most precious, life-giving gifts ever bestowed upon me. I count it a privilege to be your dad and am proud to call you handsome, intelligent, smart, respectful Black men my sons. Your presence beckons me to realms of intention forever arrested by abiding faith to actively partner with God to disciple my dreams and live a spent life.

To my best friend and mahogany queen, Christy, thank you the priceless privilege of you. Thanks for your invaluable contributions about the tone of the book. Your love and friendship have changed the trajectory of my life. You are an awesome woman and an even better person. Your blood-bought identity is simply seminal. Thank you for being more than a symbol of intention; you are an incarnation of its audacity. Selah. And oh, tell LaShaun I appreciate her too.

I want to thank LaShonda, Darrell Jr., Stasia, and Ashley for loving your son and brother with such wild abandon and fierce devotion. Thank you for the ceaseless access to your memory and history files. Thank you for vicariously co-authoring this work and for helping me craft a purposive story that promises to impact D'Anthony Marcel Jr. and the lives of others in infectious and transformative ways. I count it an honor to be your brother-in-love and uncle.

I would like to acknowledge with sincere gratitude, my publisher and editor, Chiffon R. Foster. This is our first book together. You are my childhood friend, tour guide, and destiny helper. We share birthdays, a passion for the marketplace, and a burden to be salt & light in sacred and secular spaces. You were very enthusiastic and encouraging about this project. Thanks for your invaluable contributions about the book's structure and content. You served as a doula and mid-wife throughout the birthing of this work. You provided a birth plan as well as spiritual and emotional support throughout this expecting-the-expected journey. The counseling, labor, and delivery care you provided made this birthing process memorable and empowering. Your spiritual wisdom, strategic coaching, and uninterrupted partnership have elevated my thinking and acting to a destiny decoded level.

I am surrounded by a great cloud of witnesses. Success is never individualistic or experienced in isolation. Success is created and cultivated in the bosom of community. This work is a testament to both the power and promise of communal success. There are many nameless heroes who mentored, motivated, and mobilized the writer and champion in me. This book became a reality as a result of the prayers, support, and encouragement of many individuals.

- Myles Munroe, Claudette Copeland, Spencer Conley, Robert Webb II, Chris Malone Sr., Geoffrey Dudley Sr., Chester Andrews Jr., Quenton C. Foster, Joseph Manaway, Edward Donolson III, Derwin Gray, Nina Franklin, Ralph West, Anthony R. Obey Sr., Donald Parson, Bryan Carter, Craig Brown, Karin Bronner, David Williams, Ashley Johnson, Anjanette Wilson, D'Ajah Johnson, Michael Owens, Cherie Benton, and Bam Morris for inspiring, coaching, & mentoring me in various ways along this journey. I am a grateful tributary of your spent lives.
- My mentor, Robert L. Manaway Sr., your constant presence and encouragement during the highs, lows, and in-betweens of my life cannot be quantified. Your multiplicity of selves (husband, father, pastor, friend, servant, mentor, and colleague) has provided me exemplary, timely and invaluable support. You have championed the champion in me and advised and modeled how to actualize and author intentional living in my life.
- John Klomps, who read several chapters and advised and supported me in the creation of visual aids. I will never forget how you took out an entire Saturday in a creative session.
- Johnny Taylor, who labored with me to produce the book cover designs and the final e2I model. Awesome Sauce. You gave me many great suggestions on the power of visual narration.
- Charlisha L. Greene, who patiently and intently listened to me grapple with the concepts of this book in the Dallas "transformation corner" and without fail, with an infectious outlook, encouraged me to live the dash. I so appreciate you. Your warmth, generosity, and kindness are kingdom capital.

Finally, I want to thank you, the reader. In the pages that follow, you will be called to the courageous & epic work of giving benedictions to procrastination and eventuality in order to rob the grave & reap the interest of heaven on earth. It will cost you relationships with people—including old ones with yourself—and environments who traffic in resignation, sameness, and the status quo. But what Jesus restores to you and creates through and for you will be worth it.

Patrick
Dallas, Texas

INTRODUCTION

There is a good possibility that empty dreams, unmet goals, and abandoned plans are still waiting to materialize in your life. Too much frustrated cargo is still en route to your address. I think you may agree; deferment and resignation have reigned far too long. Prayerfully this work is seen as a personal, practical, and provoking guide for you to (finally) **Move at the Speed of Intention**. The concept of **intention** is defined as *a determination to act or bring about*. **Speed** is defined as *the act or state of moving swiftly with respect to time*.

THE SPEED OF INTENTION IS CONNECTED TO PURPOSEFUL ACTIVITY THAT IS COMPELLED BY THE URGENCY OF NOW. THIS ACTIVITY IS COMFORTED BY THE CERTAINTY OF A SECURED FUTURE.

It is extremely easy to sleep walk through life! Why? Because *it is very common for people to be lulled into this lie: you have time so feel free to take your time.*

My friend, the waiting list of plans, promises, and potential continues to grow because you fail to act. Meaningful, consistent, and sustainable action on your part is on the horizon. ***The wait is waiting on you to move from procrastination to manifestation.*** Lift the weight on the wait! Aspiration (desire) requires ambition (devotion) in order to manifest. ***Your*** *future is waiting on you today. Your future will thank you for intentionally acting in your present. Every day is a new box. Open it and look at what's inside. You are the one who determines if it is a gift or a coffin.*

May 14, 2018 is a day I will never forget. *It was the day the precious life of my nephew D'Anthony Marcel Johnson, Sr. was tragically taken.* May 14th was filled and stained with conflicting feelings. On the one hand, it was stained with unspeakable pain when I received the call that his young life had been taken as a result of senseless gun violence. On the other hand, *the duality of my identity* (as Pastor and Little Brother) *wanted to offer a ministry of presence and when appropriate, bestow words of hope and comfort to his grieving and broken heart.* -The predictable *"why's"* flooded the phone lines, consumed conversations, and permeated the painful atmosphere. I immediately went into prayer. *I asked God for strength and solicited His sovereign aide to stabilize our faith, sterilize our hope, and steady our steps*. My first order of business after I prayed was to get in contact with my brother Darrell.

Even now I am moved to tears when I recall and relive the indescribable anguish my brother was in. That agonizing moment still instantly provokes weeping and worship. I can still hear the agony of his shattered heart in his broken voice as he grappled mightily to make sense of the moment. I simply listened and wept with this grieving father. I do not know how much time passed because **time has a way of standing still during moments when the soul is being scarred**. In the coming days as I sat with and listened to my big brother wrestle with the tragic loss of his oldest Prince, I could sense what Dr. Donald Parson of the Logos Baptist Assembly in Chicago, IL calls *"medicine for the moment"* and *"strategies for living"*. The medicine for the moment was introspection about his oldest son's life.

D'Anthony was certainly no saint, but he was a prince. This prince had **recalibrated his gaze, refined his focus, reenergized his passions, and reprioritized his life**. He would frequently remind and encourage his family and friends to do the same. And now he had a young son. **D'Anthony Marcel Johnson, Jr. added depth and clarity to his father's life**. His loyalty and priority now shifted to his young prince. He now had even more incentive and fuel to recalibrate, reprioritize, refine, and reenergize his gaze, life, focus, and passions. Days before his death D'Anthony told his little brother "I got it now."

He expressed to Darrell Anthony Jr. how he understood why Dad had been hard on him and why he would constantly say the things he said. D'Anthony confessed to his brother how he could not wait to tell their father how he felt and what he understood. ***Tragically, D'Anthony never got the*** *chance to utter those words to his father!* He never got the chance to express that gratefulness to their loving and devoted dad. A loving father who was now intensely grieving the expiration of his young life. ***D'Anthony, like many of us who make appointments with borrowed time***, never got the chance to convey those heartfelt sentiments to his father. ***The balance of the borrowed time unexpectedly came due.*** And the opportunity to share those confessions with his dad never came.

BUT what D'Anthony did NOT take to the grave with him was a demonstrated commitment to live… a firm resolve to move at the speed of intention and live-the-dash!!! His life is a testimony of a heart opening the new box and determining it to be a gift. His desire to be better manifested in him doing better; in being better. He was determined to act intentionally. D'Anthony did not know his young life would expire on May 14, 2018. He had no vision about when his life would end. However, he had a vision of its beginning!

Moving at the Speed of Intention was written because of my own *e2I*© (eventual to the intentional) journey. It was written because of the countless people I have come across throughout the years who have had (and continue to have) ***seasons of passive existence crippled by (1) wholesale resignation, (2) barren procrastination, (3) justified inaction, (4) chronic***

stagnation, and **(5) *sterile and unfulfilled living*.** I pray you receive clarity, comfort, competence, capacity, and confirmation from the fierce vulnerability shared in these pages. I also pray you receive hope, help, and healing for successful kingdom living from the revelation contained in this work.

Moving at the Speed of Intention is meant to empower you to RSVP to God's divine invitation to intentional living. Intention is an unwelcomed guest to sameness, convenience, and accommodation. As such, intention is an unapologetic enemy to procrastination and eventuality. ***Living-the-Dash is intentional living. And intentional living is Kingdom Living!*** It is essential to understand what I call the ***"eschatology of now"*** and view life from an eternal perspective. ***That is, live life today with eternity in mind. Your FUTURE will thank you for it TODAY!*** God has invested so much in you and has a vested interest in your success! I would be deeply honored if you allowed this book to embolden and equip you to ***live-the-dash and rob the grave; depreciating the value of the most expensive real estate on the planet***.

Moving at the Speed of Intention will inspire your capacity to be found faithful with the currency God has entrusted to your care. ***It will ignite your conviction to settle the account of your life when Jesus returns.*** It is my prayer that *Moving at the Speed of Intention* incites you to inscribe this epitaph on your tomb: ***Here lays a person who lived full and died empty***.

CHAPTER 1

EVENTUALITY VS. INTENTIONALITY

The graveyard is pregnant with the offspring of procrastination and eventuality! Their bastard seed are sterility, idleness, resignation, and convenience. Such an existence is common due to people residing in the realm of ignored possibilities, degraded priorities, and rescheduled passion.

EVENTUALITY NEVER GIVES BIRTH TO ANYTHING VIABLE AND HEALTHY

The underdeveloped and deformed DNA of postponement and aborted arrivals are irrefutable descendants of eventuality. It is a trap that lays in wait. Eventuality is not necessarily passive. Rather, in many ways it serves as an active arbiter for delay and avoidance that negotiates with your passion, productivity, and goals. Eventuality can and will never give birth to anything viable or healthy.

A birthmark of kingdom living is intentionality. Its undeniable nature is to be delivered from lifeless possibility as a calling card. Do you know how many minutes you have used up on calling cards? Back in the day we would recharge calling card minutes or desperately try to get our hands on a card that had an endless supply of minutes. ***Eventuality has been a calling card with ceaseless minutes. It is designed to keep you talking but never*** *acting*. Its inherent purpose is to keep you in the discussion room. ***Eventuality is designed to keep you in state of amusement and to never provoke your muse to movement – thinking but never doing; contemplating but never apprehending.***

Haven't you used up enough minutes on the airways of nothingness? Haven't you used up enough minutes talking about the dreams of others, but **never giving airtime to your dreams**? Are you ready to be deliberate? Are you ready to answer the call? ***Are you ready to take the call to what has been calling you? Give attention to intention! Purpose is calling!***

PURPOSE CAN BE DISRUPTIVE

Purpose can be a very disruptive force. But it is designed to be. ***If what you aspire to do or be (1) accommodates the status quo or (2) stimulates and strokes sameness, then you know intention is not involved.***

- Beware of anything that does not traffic in the currency of elevation and transformation.
- Be cautious of activity that fails to beckon desperate deliberateness in you.
- Be suspicious of invitations to accommodation and deferment.

The agenda of the past tends to keep us from the itinerary of our future. And if you are honest, ***you cannot count the times or ways you have allowed*** (a) ***pain*** or (b) misplaced ***priorities*** or (c) ***proclivities of the present*** to

sabotage your desire and ***ability*** to *see* and *seize* your ***desired future***. The diet of intention is designed to starve sameness. The language of intention is meant to disrupt convenience and transform the status quo.

One glaring example of this transformative disruption is the motivational book by Spencer Conley, a junior high and high school classmate of mine. If you want to become a better leader in your home, career, and/or community and are looking to enact positive influence that transforms and uplifts, you need to read *Lead with Love*! If you desire sameness and the status quo then you may not want to pick it up! If you do not want to put in the work to be better, then do not read it. **L**isten (chapter 2); **O**bserve (chapter 3); **V**ision (chapter 4); and **E**ducate | **E**ncourage (chapter 5) are not for the faint of heart. They are only for those who genuinely desire life-change and have an appetite for personal, and communal / corporate liberation and transformation. Do it all with L.O.V.E!

It brings me great joy to say published works like these from two Kirby Junior High alumni are in the motivational marketplace. Spencer and I are compelling, pushing, encouraging and educating our fellow humanity to be(come) better versions of ourselves. *Lead with Love* and *Moving at the Speed of Intention* are deeply rooted in and fueled by loving intention. As such, ***intention is not meant to nurse sameness or stroke accommodation***.

Intention is designed to provoke positive change! Intention deconstructs in order to create pathways for construction. (What are you building?)

Life is Pregnant With Possibilities But Will Always Remain Barren Until You Have The Courage To Accept God's Divine Invitation To Intentional Living.

The aim and charge of intention is to ***usher in discomfort to comfort***. Yes, intention is deliberately uncomfortable. And it is **always** at enmity with procrastination and eventuality.

You may be asking **"what do I do when my future is calling me, but my past is pulling on me?"**

1) Ask and believe God for strength to close the door.
2) Trust and believe God for the anointed audacity to answer the call.
3) Praise, pray, and press.
4) Walk forward in humility, expectancy, and wisdom.

Beloved, what is on the other side of "yes" is waiting for you! RSVP to the beckoning invitation of intention!

Your present is nothing more than a pit stop. It is not your dwelling place. Purpose is chasing you. Destiny is summoning you. Acknowledge the invitation. Surrender to its centripetal pull. Purpose is calling! Run to the dash! **Run into intention! Purpose is currency in the Kingdom of God.** Have the courage to give a benediction to convenience and resignation. End your relationship with accommodation for she is the mistress of these illicit affairs. ***Starve sameness. And feast on the manna of intention.***

Chapter 2

Your Move (First Steps)

Dr. Benjamin Elijah Mays: "The tragedy in life is not reaching for the stars; the tragedy in life is not having any stars to reach for. Not failure, but low aim is sin!"

The day before his death on May 13, 2018 (Mother's Day), my nephew D'Anthony expressed this to his little brother Darrell Jr…

- What needed to be done (1. as a big brother; 2. as the first and oldest son; 3. as a father)
- About the bigger picture (to show others how it needs to be done; wanted to be an example and to lead by example).
- How important it was to be a step up and be a man.
- How to stop doing the same things repeatedly.
- It was okay to be better and do better.
- It was okay to turn the corner.
- Not to try to prove anything to anybody, but to simply embrace identity and to let identity drive decisions.

D'Anthony discovered that ***"you cannot live above the revelation you have of yourself"*** (Foster, 2018, p. 5). You could be reading this book and think this was a new revelation. A revelation that had not had any liftoff because it had just taxied to the runway of his life. The truth is the May 13th conversation had incubated for more than two years in his bosom. You see, D'Anthony had just been released from jail after serving the previous two years. ***Before he had gone to jail this young prince had already begun recalibrating his gaze, refining his focus, and reprioritizing his life.***

Don't Count Time

The decision to make time count rather than just count time was well into motion. It had traveled down the runway and already had liftoff. The trajectory of the liftoff was so powerful that D'Anthony had turned himself in to the authorities for a parole violation. He had already devoted himself to his renewed mindset. ***He did not want his violation to imprison his victory.*** He made the most of his **isolation** and used it for **excavation** and **elevation**. ***He elevated his thinking so that he could elevate his acting. He let his mindset and motives marinate in order to season his next season.*** My nephew decided to accept God's invitation to intentional living.

His conduct was in covenant with his confession. In other words, his identity (belief) gave birth to intention (behavior). This is not revisionist history of an imperfect life or a feeble attempt to rewrite his life's story to make it more palatable for the consumption of those he left behind. So that family, friends, and loved ones can coalesce around a warm fire to find comfort in a fabricated narrative. This is not a posthumous proclamation and sanitized spin appearing after the death of my nephew to sterilize his life. ***He did not just discover who he was*** (his identity was not unknown); he

uncovered (identity was hidden) and ***recovered*** (identity was lost) who he was. ***Time then became a currency that his identity spent on living.*** What a powerful life lesson! What do you need to *discover **about*** yourself? What do you need to *uncover **in*** yourself? What do you need to *recover **for*** yourself?

The sunset of my nephew's earthly life tragically ended on May 14, 2018.

- One can say the sunrise of his life began on May 10, 1992 when his loving mother gave birth to him.
- Or one could say his life began the moment his parents conceived his existence around August 1991.
- Or one could say his life began before he was formed in his mother's womb (see Jeremiah 1:5; Galatians 1:15; Isaiah 44:2, 24; Psalm 139:13-16).

Whichever date or date range is selected to indicate the ***beginning of his life***, it does not illustrate when he exercised the audacity to move at the speed of intention and live-the-dash! ***The decision to make time count rather than just count time ushers us into the realm of intention.***

MAKE TIME COUNT

Like D'Anthony (and for that matter like many Biblical characters), despite where you came from and even despite where you start… and like many others who unfortunately share the headstone of premature exits and unannounced expiration dates, here are 10 things you should do to make your time in this life count:

1) Seize the present and thoughtfully and deliberately lean into your future. *Exercise the 'then' now*.
2) Nurture a covenant relationship between your conduct and your confession. *Elevate your thinking in order to elevate your acting.*
3) *Do not allow violations to imprison your victory.*
4) *Practice and possess peace even when the present is tense.*
5) *Understand the virtue and value of isolation.*
6) Make *mindsets* and *motives marinate* in order to *season* your next season.
7) Calibrate your life and diet. *If it is not congruent with your future it should not be palatable in your present.*
8) Grasp that **manifestation of promise is released when** *realization* **and** *readiness* **are** *rehearsed.*
9) **Divorce eventuality.** *Your future is auditioning IN your present.*
10) **Marry intentionality.** *Your present is auditioning FOR your future.*

These 10 principles are not just medicine for the moment. They are strategies for living. They are strategies required to **stop making appointments with borrowed time**. Practicing these principles are required to truly accept God's invitation to intentional living.

Do Not Say Yes and Do No

The day before his tragic death my nephew confessed, and in the prior two years demonstrated, that he **refused to let his past memories paralyze his present or master his future**. D'Anthony had been guilty of what Bishop (Dr.) Geoffrey V. Dudley, Sr. of the New Life in Christ Interdenominational Church in O'Fallon, IL calls the **"say yes and do no"** cycle of sameness. My beloved nephew had *'said yes'* and *'did no'* in his past. However, he had now utterly refused to believe he would be stuck in repeat. D'Anthony had decided to live and move at the speed of intention. **He had served his time, now time was serving him**. He had served his time so he could get on with his new lease on life and live his dash.

No doubt it would do us well to acknowledge the elephant in the room: D'Anthony Sr. tragically died at the young age of 26; a mere 4 days after his birthday. One of the stated regrets of his loving parents is they will not get to see him raise his son (D'Anthony Marcel Johnson, Jr.). They will not get to witness their son grow into an old man or see how his life would have turned out now that he had turned the corner and allowed God to turn his life around. Yes, those things are a minor dataset and representation of the mass data points of examples that can fill the bucket of regret. However, there is much to be grateful for. The thankful list cannot only fill the bucket of gratefulness; it can overflow it! *And the medicine for the moment of his grieving father and mother is turning their (our) mourning into dancing.*

MOURNING INTO DANCING

In Psalm 30:10-12 the Prophet Gad had brought David some joyful news. Upon delivery of the news, he commanded David to build an altar to God. The Bible says when David built the altar, the mourning ceased. The Lord had empowered and provoked David to peel (throw) off his sackcloth (worn in times of calamity and distress and sometimes as a token of humiliation and repentance) and girded him with gladness.

David discovered that God was not hiding His face nor was God's hand amputated from his struggle. *His life had been restored from the pit* (Ps. 30:3). He *celebrated both the justice and joy of God* (Ps. 30:5). *He plead for mercy and help* (Ps. 30:2, 8, 10). *David's morning came when his mourning ceased* (Ps. 30:11a). He was girded with gladness when his *isolation gave way to elevation* (Ps. 30:11b). Silence was unmuted and *thanks poured in in response to God's presence* (Ps. 30:7) *and mercy* (Ps. 30:12). Darrell Anthony Johnson, Sr. and my sister-in-love LaShonda McCloud (the loving and devoted parents of my nephew) teach us that the medicine for the moment can become strategies for living. *Introspection can become helium*

to hurt, food for the soul, and fuel for your faith. Like Prince D'Anthony M. Johnson Sr.,

- Recalibrate your gaze
- Refine your focus
- Reenergize your passion(s)
- Reprioritize your life

Dr. Chiffon R. Foster is my great friend who also serves as a tour guide and destiny helper in my life. In her life changing book *Destiny Decoded* she declared, "Your destiny is calling you. Will you answer the call?" (Foster, 2018, p. 47). Are you going to answer the call? Are you going to accept God's invitation? Or are you going to continue to cancel your reservation with intentional living?

CHAPTER 3

CANCELLED RESERVATIONS

Edwin Louis Cole: "Your best friend and worst enemy are both in the room right now. It's not your neighbor to your right or left. And it's not God or the devil. It's you."

Insufficient time and space exists for me to tell you how many times *'would of / could of / should of'* have testified on my behalf! To add, I cannot count the number of people I have encountered who have been infected by the environment of sameness, apathy, and resignation.

- I can't tell you how many people I know who are crippled with *immobility, inactivity,* and *idleness.*
- I have interacted with countless people who are choosing to *sleep walk through life* and refuse to be shaken from the *slumber of passive existence.*
- Can you number the people (include yourself in the count) plagued by the diseases of sterile procrastination and barren intention?

In this ecosystem, *eventuality* has become the main course and principal diet with *intentionality* perpetually offered as an off-menu selection. We are all confronted with the nagging cross examination of life! We all approach **"the why"** for living in different ways. None of us can escape this particular universal inquiry and examination: **will we answer the call and say yes to *living full and dying empty*?** I pray this book bolsters your courage and deepens your conviction **not to disregard or dishonor the**

dignity and destiny of your life. Pull gifts and purposes off life support! Pull off the grave clothes! Snatch unfulfilled purpose, untapped potential, and unreleased possibility out of the grave! On an EKG it shows the levels of life. Can't you feel your pulse indicating your desire to live intentionally?

My sincere hope is we all learn to deliberately and actively partner with God to depreciate the value of "the most expensive real estate on the planet" (Munroe, 1991, p. 13). This book is written to encourage and equip you to:

- ❖ Rob the grave of dishonored and canceled reservations scheduled by eventuality.
- ❖ Rob the grave of the empty and unfilled transactions processed by procrastination.
- ❖ Be evicted from living and operating in the dimension of *would of / could of / should of.*
- ❖ Eulogize 'saying yes' and 'doing no'.
- ❖ Embrace confessions and conduct that stain the soul and incentivize living.

It is only when we accept the divine invitation to **Move at the Speed of Intention** that we can **Live-the-Dash.** When we accept it God will grant us the courage, capacity, and competence to **(1)** resign from resignation, **(2)** convert idleness to God-inspired usefulness, **(3)** give a benediction to convenience, and **(4)** breach our lease with eventuality.

GET OUT

Breaking this lease triggers eviction from the domains of regret, procrastination, and passive existence. In the Season 2 finale of the HBO hit series *Insecure* the therapist gave Molly Carter some wonderful advice. ***The life-changing counsel she gave to a fictional character was anything but fictional and easily becomes art imitating life***. In the season finale the therapist encouraged Molly (and us) to **"get out of *the could* and get into *the should.*"** Remember, your future is auditioning in your present. And your present is auditioning for your future. Get out of *the could* and into *the should*. Robbing the most expensive real estate on the planet demands it.

CHAPTER 4

RSVP TO GOD'S INVITATION

ESPN's Stuart Scott: "Don't downgrade your dream to fit your reality. Upgrade your conviction to match your destiny."

Time is a gift! My matter-of-fact mother has never been accused of sugar coating anything. During a conversation on my 46th birthday she said, "If you are in the land of the living then you get a birthday every year. Another year has been added to the dash. You are aging and time is winding." Amen Mamma! *With each new dawn we have one day less to live; we are one day nearer the grave. So, time is precious!*

- In Psalm 39:4-5 David said *"You have made my days a mere handbreadth; the span of my years is as nothing before you.* Each man's life is but a breath".

- In the conclusion of the Book of James, the Apostle challenges us not to boast about tomorrow nor to make appointments with borrowed time: [13] Come now, you who say, "Today or tomorrow we will go into such and such a town and spend a year there and trade and make a profit"— [14] yet you do not know what tomorrow will bring. **What is your life?** *For you are a mist that* **appears for a little time** *and* **then vanishes**. [15] Instead you ought to say, "If the Lord wills, we will live and do this or that." (James 4:13-15, English Standard Version of the Bible).

In Ephesians 5:15-16 the Apostle Paul exhorts us to "Be very careful, then, **how you live**—not as unwise but as wise, **making the most of every opportunity**, because the days are evil." Conley (2017) echoed this principle when he penned, "Life is about purpose and maximizing that purpose as much as we can before we expire" (p. 49). So, time is not only precious! *It is also perishable*! Time is a non-renewable commodity and perishable resource that God invites (implores) us to use intentionally.

We should not take this precious resource of time for granted. Familiarity can (and often does) breed contempt. When we hear "don't take time for granted" it tends to sound quaint, lacking the urgency of now. And it may even sound religious or rehearsed. But it is the truth: **we are indeed living on borrowed time!**

Conley (2017) summons this plain and undeniable truth. We do suffer from what he calls "a crippling disconnect." That is, we struggle with embracing the reality that this life is not forever. "You would think we all would value time and live to the fullest. Yet we hide behind fantasy and denial" (Conley, 2017, p. 100). It is essential we **make the best possible use of our allotted time**. When will we stop...

1) Divorcing our individual and collective consciousness from the beckoning gift of the present?

2) Robing our frail humanity in disarming, comfortable, complacent, and even arrogant denial?
3) Rejecting God's loving and lifting, patient yet persistent invitation to live with intentionality?
4) Passively and ignorantly refusing to live life on purpose and with purpose?

"Understanding fuels change" (Conley, 2017, p. 36). Do we really understand that we are living on borrowed time? Do we truly grasp that we will have to give an account of what we did with the time God has gifted to us? When will we accept that we are indeed living on time that has both been (a) borrowed from the Father of it and (b) gifted to us? ***If we understand it then it is time to stand under it!*** It is time to change our language and to update our diet.

THE DIET & LANGUAGE OF INTENTION

Dr. Chiffon Rena Foster is right! **"Preparedness attracts favor from the throne room and in the market place."** It sends smoke signals to heaven declaring a stewardship of readiness. There is profound and practical merit to the preparation mandate. **How can we pray for God to open doors if we are not prepared to sit at the table?** In one of our many engaging and thought-provoking thought experiments, Dr. Foster reminded me that "tables represent conversations and chairs represent positions." Therefore, we need to have relationships with others who are fluid in the dialect of destiny. Selah.

People fluid in the dialect of destiny are bilingual. That is they can speak in the vernacular of your present and converse in the language of your future. They can either prepare or point you to meals that are *suitable for your diet of intention*. "You must get fed at the level of your future… For you to be sustained as you move from level to level, you will need food FROM your future. The person (or environment) that is feeding you must be FROM the place they are trying to take you to" (Foster, 2018, p. 37).

Environments and relationships matter! They are lifeline to your future. They give clarity, context, and content for your present. They also serve as mile markers so that you better understand if you are moving in the right direction. Environments and relationships help to condition your passion. Connections and atmospheres truly do matter. *If they do not stretch you then I question their validity, veracity, and value. They should always be stimulating, challenging, and upgrading you.* The saying is true, "If you look at the people in your circle and do not get inspired then you do not have a circle, you have a cage." My football teammate at Texas Tech University and the leading rusher in Super Bowl XXX said it better than I ever could. Byron "Bam" Morris shared, "If you're hanging out with somebody and they're not going in the same direction you are, you need to drop them off. Because you're going to get into trouble. And that's what I couldn't do. I could never drop them off. And that's a reason why I had a wreck" (Bradford, 2016, para 42). ***Who and/or what do you need to drop off?***

Environments and relationships should be compelling you to actively partner with God in manifesting your preferred future. If they are worth their weight in gold, they should be encouraging and equipping you to schedule time with intention. Healthy environments and relationships should embolden you to ***create spaces for the canvas of your imagination to be painted on***. That in and of itself is being intentional. ***Create spaces chartered by intention and it will manifest intentionality and give life to the offspring of procrastination and eventuality.***

"The Dash" (2019) is a powerful poem penned by a great writer and poet. I hope this poem inspires you in the same way it continues to both inspire and ignite my life.

"The Dash" by Linda Ellis

I read of a man who stood to speak at a funeral of a friend. He referred to the dates on the tombstone from the beginning... to the end.

He noted that first came the date of birth and spoke of the following date with tears, but he said what mattered most of all was the dash between those years.

For that dash represents all the time they spent alive on earth and now only those who loved them know what that little line is worth.

For it matters not, how much we own, the cars... the house... the cash. What matters is how we live and love and how we spend our dash.

So, think about this long and hard; are there things you'd like to change? For you never know how much time is left that still can be rearranged.

To be less quick to anger and show appreciation more and love the people in our lives like we've never loved before.

If we treat each other with respect and more often wear a smile... remembering that this special dash might only last a little while.

So, when your eulogy is being read, with your life's actions to rehash, would you be proud of the things they say about how you lived your dash?

CHAPTER 5

INHALE PURPOSE. EXHALE DESTINY.

Barbara Joyce Brown-Henry (my mother): "Don't stumble over yourself by trying to be someone you are not. And don't stumble in life by not living out who you are."

Dr. Myles Munroe was right, the most expensive real estate on the planet is not the diamond mines of South Africa. It is not the oil fields of Iran, Iraq or Kuwait. Nor is it the uranium mines of the Soviet Union. Out of curiosity I researched some of the world's most expensive real estate based on 2018 market values. ***They would not even serve as an adequate down payment to purchase the most expensive real estate on the planet.***

- The Grande Estate on Indian Creek Island in Dade County, FL. Cost, $35M
- The French country estate in Saint Tropez, France. Cost, $35M
- A hotel apartment in Dubai. Cost, $69M
- The Phillimore Gardens in London - the entire house is covered with marble and gold. Cost, $128M
- The Hearst Castle in San Simeon, CA - 56 bedrooms; world's largest private zoo. Cost, $195M
- The Fairfield Pond estate in NY - 21 bedrooms, 18baths, garage holds up to 100 cars. Cost, $248M
- The largest & most expensive French Villa in the world... once owned by King Leopold II of Belgium. Cost, $750M
- The Antilia (a private house in South Mumbai, India) - consists of 27 floors, 6 underground parking floors, 3 helicopter pads, and a fulltime staff of 600 people. Cost, $1B

The most expensive and wealthiest place in the world are not gold mines or oil fields or diamond mines or banks. It is not these opulent estates, gardens, or villas. *The most expensive real estate on the planet is the cemetery* (Munroe, 1991). Buried in the graveyard are:

- **companies never started**
- **books never written**
- **masterpieces never painted**
- **words never spoken**
- **dreams that were never fulfilled**
- **ideas that never became reality**
- **visions that were never manifested**
- **songs never penned**
- **decisions never made**
- **potential never released**
- **concepts never pursued and**
- **time never given**

Dr. Myles Munroe was a tremendous gift to humanity. His published works on leadership, manhood, and purpose are transformative gems. He was perfectly precise. *The cemetery is pregnant with unused success. Buried in the cemetery are treasures that make God weep.* YES, the God of the universe weeps!

THE GOD WHO WEEPS AND WAITS

Two occasions are recorded in the Gospels of Jesus weeping: **1).** At the gravesite of Lazarus (see John 11:35) and **2).** His last trip to Jerusalem before His crucifixion (see John 19:41). The first occasion of Jesus weeping is unsurprising because He had just spoken with Mary and Martha (John 11:19-32), Lazarus's grief-stricken sisters. On the other hand, the fact that Jesus was weeping is startling because He came to Bethany for the sole purpose of raising Lazarus from the dead (John 11:11, 23); knowing He could have stopped Lazarus from dying (John 11:12-15, 37).

The truth of the text teaches us that Jesus knew the **weeping would soon turn to astonished joy** after He raised Lazarus from the dead. **So why did Jesus weep?** Jesus did not weep because of the death of Lazarus. Jesus knew He would soon raise Lazarus and he would ultimately spend eternity with Him **(I. Lazarus's Future was Secured)**. Jesus wept because of His **(a)** *compassion for suffering* (God identifies with those *who experience lost*).

Luke 19:41-44 chronicles the second recorded occasion of Jesus weeping. In this instance, Jesus wept over the condition of those in Jerusalem. The inhabitants in Jerusalem rejected the good news and those who brought it (see Luke 13:34). Jesus wept because of the **(b)** *calamity of* *sin* (God identifies with those *who are lost*). Christ cried aloud in anguish over the future of the city **(II. Their Future was Sorrowful)**.

Jesus wept differently on these two occasions. The eternal outcomes were in stark contrast. They were completely different because Lazarus, Mary, and Martha trusted in Jesus and had the gift of eternal life. Most in Jerusalem rejected Jesus and were denied the gift of eternal life. *Is your future secure? Or is your future sorrowful?* Is Jesus weeping because of His compassion for your suffering? Or is He weeping because of the calamity of sin?

Is Jesus Weeping Because You Are Taking All The Stuff He Has Invested In You To The Grave?

- Do not make God weep because your life lacks passion, engagement, and meaning (Ephesians 1:11; Philippians 2:4, 3:9-10; Ecclesiastes 12:13-14).
- Do not make God weep because you are wandering aimlessly through life not experiencing His help and refusing to rest in the shadow of His wings (Psalm 63:7).
- Do not make God weep in response to not living in the fullness of His purpose for you (1 Peter 2:9; Acts 13:36; Ephesians 2:10).

Dr. Ralph Douglas West offered the Sovereign's weeping subscription in his April 4, 2019 devotional:

"Just because God is invisible doesn't mean He is unknowable. In fact, He desires for you to know His character and see His work in your life. God is saying, "I have made an investment in every one of you, and I am looking for something in your life in return. I want you to mature, produce, and be fruitful.""

Ask God for wisdom and direction (James 1:5). Trust the Wonderful, Counselor (Isaiah 9:6) for your direction in life (Psalm 119:105). God will help you identify and/or resurrect your gifts and highlight where they intersect with your passions. God is weeping because you are experiencing loss. God is weeping because you are lost. ***Do not take unused success with you to the cemetery. Inhale purpose and exhale destiny!*** Do not bury the treasures of undiscovered identity and untapped intention with you in the graveyard. *Let the Lord add super to your natural!*

CHAPTER 6

LIVING IN THE KEY OF LIFE: B NATURAL

Let me start this chapter off by saying I am not a musician. I love music and took my one and only music class in 6th grade at Edgar Allen Poe Middle School. It would be great to learn to play the organ and piano one day! Calls have been made to friends of mine regarding that life goal. Hopefully musical maestros like Donyea (Dwight) Goodman, Robert E. Webb II, Rockell Scott, Chester Andrews Jr., Cleophus Robinson III, Aristide Brown Jr., and Charles Ransom II will take me on as student one day.

I sincerely encourage you to watch and listen to the interview Dr. Frank A. Thomas conducted with one of my preaching heroes, Dr. Claudette Anderson Copeland. He is the Director of the Academy of Preaching and Celebration and Professor of Homiletics at the Christian Theological Seminary (CTS) in Indianapolis, Indiana. In 2016, CTS launched a **PhD program in African American Preaching and Sacred Rhetoric**. The Association of Theological Schools (ATS) accredited it as the first PhD program in African American Preaching in the world. Dr. Thomas engaged in a soul watering interview with Dr. Copeland for the African American Preaching Legacy Series (Frank, 2017).

It was this conversation that inspired my thinking about this chapter. Of the many things Dr. Claudette Copeland spoke about in this life changing interview:

1. **"The lifelong yes"** to ministry and life.
2. The importance of **"reading the fine print"** to the invitation of God on your life.
3. **"Placement and symbols matter and send powerful messages to those who watch and see,"** but resting in the authenticity of God's hand on your life transcends and reshapes borders and redefines identity and its efficacy in sacred spaces.
4. Most of her **mentors** are names most people won't even know. **It is not their notoriety, but their nature that activated and actualized her call and ministry.** It is their "authentic connection to that which is unseen" that arrests, propels, and transforms. **Mentors situate you where your voice can be heard and confirm** (authenticate) **what God is doing and wants to do in your life.**
5. Learning is God's gift to your life.
6. Studying Pastoral Care was **her way of trying to heal herself** and did not even realize she was gravitated towards it because she had **"learned to play hurt"** (athletic imagery).
7. **"How have you used your injuries?"** / **"How have you used this substance and soul for your own life?"**
8. "Admitting the antithesis" of your declarations and beliefs may **"cut across the grain of your own truth." Admit it and then give it audience to what Jesus says**. Expose it to possibilities and the

existence of a higher truth; something against your own injury and resistance.

9. **Consider and wrestle with the "Potter's Prerogative"** (see Romans 9:20-21). In discussing the textual excavation and excavations of life she posited how we, like Paul, have exclaimed, **"I don't want my pain to deform me."** She bellowed the cry of the Apostle Paul from this text. And affirmed we share this same cry: **"God why did You make me this way?!?"**
10. **Substance and the stage are not always in concert.** Have enough humility to **examine your blind spots** and **do not be resistant to mirrors.**

Of the litany of soul stirring areas Dr. Copeland covered in this 1 hour and 8 minute interview, **it was around the 29 minute mark that she incited my thinking about this book chapter**.

Dr. C. (as she is affectionately called) talked about *"Preaching in the Key of F: The Key of Femininity."* She championed and celebrated the great value of this key. She expressed the tragedy of trading such value in for a model that is antithetical to its virtue. **"When presented healthily you don't have to use it** (identity) **as some kind of stage bait."** The importance of not exchanging the currency of your virtue and value for the applause or acceptance of others cannot be overstated.

"Genuinely utilizing the substance and soul of your own life" will continually escape you if you fail to RSVP to God's invitation to intentional living. According to Dr. Claudette A. Copeland, it is when we accept such an invitation that the *"incarnational nature of the Spirit stirs it up like good butter, flower, sugar, and milk so that the cake you offer is really good cake."* This good cake is another way of saying to <u>**live in the key of life**</u>. **Live into your authenticity healthily. Do not trade it in for acceptance or convenience. Do not use it as stage bait.** The sole purpose of bait it to lure and trap. **Be authentic.** This will ensure you are not on the end of the hook. God wants to use you to love, lift, and cure.

Craft a magnum opus from life's notes and melodies for intentional living. This work of art will be your most important work. With the keen help of maestros Robert E. Webb II and Chester Andrews Jr., I pray you effectively discern some key lessons to *Living in the Key of Life*. May they propel your lifelong journey of intentional living to higher heights.

CHROMATIC SCALES

In the chromatic scale there are a total of 13 potential keys. This scale has one repeating key that is higher or lower than the starting key. This acts as the starting or ending point for each ensuing scale. The sound of some keys—although visually appearing the same and called a different name as it is associated with its relative signature—sound the same (for example, C-sharp sounds the same as D-flat). Whether higher or lower than the starting key, the key in each scale is played the same way and sounds identical.

> *LESSON 1:* IT IS DIFFICULT TO DECIPHER YOUR SOUND
> WHEN YOU EMULATE THE SOUND OF OTHERS.
> IT IS DIFFICULT TO DETERMINE YOUR DESTINY
> WHEN IT'S BEEN ASSIMILATED BY OTHER NOTES.

Living in the Key of Life creates **scales** (set of notes ordered by either an ascending or descending pitch). And you must be mindful of the fundamental frequency and sound they give. What chromatic scales exist in your life? **What sound is your life making?** Is the sound of your life sharp (denoted by a '#' symbol)? Or is it flat (super scripted by a 'b' symbol)? **Is your life being played in a sharp key or in a flat key?** Is your key signature # or b? Have you moved above or below your starting key?

KEY SIGNATURE

Robert Webb was so kind to explain to me that "all of us begin our lives in a key with no sharps or flats… sharps (**moments of danger or extreme excitement**); flats (**low moments**)." In the chromatic scale there are 5 additional notes known as **"accidentals"** or simply called **"sharps"** (which raise the original sound of the note) and **"flats"** (which lower the original sound of the note). I almost hollered when he explained this and broke it down to me! Accidental notes = sharps and flats.

LESSON 2: WHETHER WE INTERPRET AND EXPERIENCE THE EVENTS OF LIFE AS A HIGH (SHARP) OR A LOW (FLAT), THEY ARE INCLUDED IN THE KEY SIGNATURE OF OUR LIVES.

KEY OF C

Maestro Webb is right:

> "**All of us begin life in the Key of C**, which has no sharps or flats. Our lives experience Major Chords (happy, joyful sounding melodies). As we age, we gradually move away from the Key of C to a different key. **Life happens!** And as the key changes so does the signature. As the key signature changes—**which adds to the ever-evolving complexity of life by the addition of accidentals**—so does the fingering for the scale. We, while attempting to maintain the Major (happy, joyful) sound of the scale of life, we not only have to adjust our hand position (**stretch our commitment and capacity**); we also have to **adjust our mental and visual position**."

LESSON 3: TO LIVE IN THE KEY OF LIFE YOU MUST INTENTIONALLY ADJUST FOR THE ACCIDENTALS YOU EXPERIENCE.

Many times this involves stretching to change your current position or existing condition. In music—just as in life—to change keys, the position must change. And this demands stretching and learning a new methodology or process to achieve a new objective. Move out of your comfort zone. End your relationship with complacency and the familiar.

MASTERING ACCIDENTAL NOTES

The prophetic voice of Robert E. Webb II is clearly heard in his musicology:

> "We must now always be mindful of the accidental (situation or circumstance) that has been introduced. We must maintain an intentional bent toward its mastery or navigation. **Familiarity with the accidental will allow for greater facility and functionality**... The greater the number of accidentals, the greater the degree of complexity of the fingering.
>
> Failure to make these adjustments are guaranteed to result in a less than happy sounding scale. **Failure to make the appropriate adjustments in positioning, vision, and mindset will result in a more than difficult and less than happy life."**

Theologically we master accidentals by going to the Master Composer of Life. Jesus is both the *pre-existent* (see John 1:1-18; 17:5; 8:3, 58-59; Colossians 1:16-17) and *ever-present* (see Psalm 46:1; 91:14-16; 18:6-19; 145:18; Jeremiah 23:23-24; Acts 17:27-28; Matthew 28:20) Maestro and Teacher.

It is from the tutelage of God and our trust in Him that we learn to master and navigate life.

Musically the accidentals are mastered by remembering them. For example, in the Key of C all white keys are played and no accidentals exist. However, when B-flat is played accidentals exist. B*b* and E*b* must be remembered. The accidentals are mastered by knowing if any additional accidentals make an appearance. They are only valid if they are notated as such by the previous occurrence. According to Maestro Webb,

> **"Accidentals are temporary deviations from an established key signature. The best way to deal with the accidental is to acknowledge it.** Play it and remember it as it may become part of a recurring sub theme necessary to articulate the intended message of the composer. Case in point, the Apostle Paul asked again and again for God to remove the thorn from his flesh (see 2 Corinthians 12:8). God's response was that His grace was sufficient to and for him (see 2 Corinthians 12:9)."

One of the things I find to be an insightful nugget for Living in the Key of Life is that **Paul acknowledged the very real possibility he knew the *purpose behind his thorn*** **and understood the *purpose of his pain*.** He needed to boast about his weaknesses (see 2 Corinthians 12:5) and to counteract being conceited (see 2 Corinthians 12:7). The Apostle Paul realized the benefit of not thinking too highly of himself for in doing so he would not forget the source, resource, and sustainer of life.

> *LESSON 4:* WE ARE DIRECT BENEFACTORS OF THE UNMERITED AND FREE FAVOR OF GOD. CHRIST TOLD PAUL (AND US) THAT HIS GRACE IS SUFFICIENT TO HANDLE THE SHARPS AND FLATS OF LIFE.

We are recipients of divine endowment and provision. **His grace is sufficient to keep life in the Key of C (free from accidentals) and even during accidentals**. My good friend and brother Chester Andrews, Jr. is a musical savant. One would hard be pressed to find a more sincere, humble, gifted, and multifaceted (teacher, expositor, writer, producer, engineer, accompanist) leader in sacred or secular spaces today. Chester shared this powerful life application nugget with me: **"Like the Apostle Paul, it is critical that we acknowledge the accidentals in our lives so that our scales result in the Divine Composer's intended sound."**

Christ not only promised us through Paul that His grace is sufficient **(more than enough)**; He promised **His all-sufficient strength is made perfect** in our weakness / frailty / imperfection (see 2 Corinthians 12:9). The *"dynamis"* of God (New Testament Greek word for **power** in verse 9) is **connected to you**! It is the root word of our English words *dyn*amite, *dyn*amo, and *dyn*amic. Dynamis, pronounced dunamis (doo-nam-is), is inherent in the very nature of God (see Matthew 22:29; 24:30; Luke 4:36; Romans 1:20; 2 Corinthians 4:7). **And this power is available and afforded to you**. Christian Scripture teaches that we cannot accomplish anything of value apart from God (see John 15:1-5).

LESSON 5: YOU CANNOT AND DO NOT LIVE LIFE IN (ON) YOUR OWN POWER. APART FROM GOD WE CAN DO NOTHING.
THE POWER OF GOD IS NOT ONLY <u>DYNAMITE</u>;
IT MAKES YOU <u>DYNAMIC</u>!

> Ephesians 3:20-21 "Now to Him who is able to do immeasurably more than all we ask or imagine, according to His **power** that is at work within us, to Him be glory in the church and in Christ Jesus throughout all generations, for ever and ever! Amen." (New International Version translation of the Bible)

> 2 Peter 1:3 "His divine **power** has given us everything we need for a godly life through our knowledge of him who called us by his own glory and goodness."
> (New International Version translation of the Bible)

Listen to the Apostle Paul's testimony about how he learned to **Live in the Key of Life**: *"That is why for Christ's sake I delight in (well content with) weaknesses, in insults, in hardships, in persecutions, in difficulties. For* *when I am weak than am I strong"* (see 2 Corinthians 9:10). **How you deal with accidentals determines everything. Accidentals can be purposeful and transformative.** They can force you to change your **position, perspective**, and **practice. Accidentals can also (re)condition your** *outlook* **on life and subsequently change the** *outcomes* **of (in) life.**

B NATURAL

Appendix A in this book chronicles some additional notes from the piano bench. Robert E. Webb III was very kind and thoughtful in his engagement. He humbly made himself available the moment I announced my interest in tapping his musical genius and passion in my quest to shape some intentional living life lessons from them. Specifically, I communicated my desire to grasp some key musical concepts aligned with the purpose of this work. The stated goal was to fashion a lived opus from aspects of musical theory. An opus filled with notes, melodies, and movements to glance the mind and touch the soul; resulting in informed and inspired living. Did he ever deliver!

There are many additional **Life Lessons** contained in the appendix dedicated to his notes from the vantage point of a concert pianist. I highly encourage you to review them. They are truly life changing. Webb discusses the power of patterns and chord progression, chord symbolism in Western musicology, and melodic successes and failures. The life lesson focused on in this chapter section is Maestro Webb's discussion on the **Key of B Natural**.

> "There is a system known as the Circle of 4th's (for flats) and a similar system known as the Circle of 5th's (for sharps) which states that **within each step of the Circle an additional accidental is added to the Key Signature**.
>
> One of the most difficult Key Signatures for many keyboardists is the **Key of B Natural.** It is difficult because everything is seemingly an accidental. However, following the circle of 4th's or 5th's prepares you for the daunting task of playing in the Key of B Natural.
>
> **Once you have become a virtuoso in all the other keys, having mastered the use of all the accidentals, then it becomes natural for you to play in B Natural.** It is neither flat nor sharp.
>
> **B Natural**—while represented by the 5 sharps in B natural (C#, D#, F#, G#, A#)—**still maintains the unaltered natural pattern of the major scale**. Thus, with proper practice and consistency of form, the nightmare of dealing with the accidentals (along with the potential of others for the sake of melodic inflection) becomes a Mid Summer's Night dream like the Key of C, having not one accidental in sight."

THANK YOU, Robert E. Webb, for these marvelous excavations from the piano bench!

The Master's Masterpiece

Living in the Key of Life means you must **master the accidentals**. Remember, **accidentals are temporary deviations from the key signature The Master Composer has established for your life.** Continue to acknowledge the accidentals and learn from them. Become a victorious virtuoso and master the use of all the accidentals in your life. **The unaltered pitch of the notes of your life can be *recovered*. B Natural. Be intentional. The unaltered pitch of the notes of your life can also be *discovered*.**

Dr. (Professor) Edward Donalson III, Director of the Doctor of Ministry Program at Seattle University, is one of my beloved brothers in ministry and the academy. This thought leader and public theologian summarized this as the need to "engage life from a centered core that cancels the effects of major and minor transitions." The Master Composer has a plan and purpose for your life. So, accept God's invitation.

Live in the Key of Life. Rob the Grave. Depreciate its Value. Live Full. Die Empty. **Discover and/or recover the music and melodies the Master Composer and Conductor has ordained for you. You are His magnum opus!**

God knows the exact sounds, timing, and rhythms of your life. It is unfolding perfectly.

- There is harmony *to* **your life**.
- There is harmony *in* **your life**.
- There is harmony *for* **your life**.

Embrace the rhythm of your life. Honor the Master Composer. Relentlessly pursue this truth. **Embrace God's identity for you. You are His masterpiece!**

> LEARN THE NOTES AND MUSIC GOD HAS DESIGNED FOR YOU TO PLAY. GOD DESIRES THE SOUND EMITTING FROM THE COMPOSITION OF YOUR LIFE TO BE PLEASING TO HIM.

Ephesians 2:10 "For we are God's masterpiece. He has created us anew in Christ Jesus, so we can do the good things he planned for us long ago." (New Living Translation of the Bible)

Chapter 7

The Testimony Of Tattoos

One of the many life lessons my nephew D'Anthony taught us is marking life so we can leave a mark on life. I chuckle now as I relive the story his loving mother shared with me as she grieved and celebrated his life. LaShonda is such a great story teller! During the early stages of her mourning she reminisced about D'Anthony receiving his first tattoo. See the thing is he was aware his mother does not particularly care for tats. So, he created a way to ease her potential disappointment. Better yet, D'Anthony *intentionally* created a way for his mother to exchange her misgivings for the gift he was giving her.

In a very animated way—LaShonda (to know her is to love her… her laugh is **as big** as her warm heart)—told me how D'Anthony broke the news of his first tattoo. Now recall LaShonda ***does not care at all*** for tattoos and was far from shy in expressing this to her children. So, when her first born son broke the news (I am giggling now!), D'Anthony informed her that he did indeed get a tattoo. And LaShonda recollected to me how unhappy she was with his decision. But then something happened!!! D'Anthony eagerly revealed **his first tattoo was one with her face and name on it.** HA! WOW! **He intentionally stained and branded his body with his loving mother's** *name and face on it!* LaShonda's grief turned into gladness and her mourning into laughter when she remembered what her son had done.

> **Note:** this book is not a treaty for or against tattoos (see 1 Corinthians 10:23, 31; 9:22-23; Romans 14:23; Leviticus 19:28; 1 Corinthians 6:19-20; 2 Corinthians 5:20; 1 Peter 3:3-4; and James 1:5 for the religious discussion).

Death has a way of making all of us captive audiences as it confronts our finite existence, exposes our frailty, and reminds us of our humanity. These realities also invite us to *stop counting time* and quicken us to *start making time count*. God created time when He created the universe. *Time is the indefinite progress of existence.* This existence is measured in seconds… in hours… in minutes… in moments… in days, weeks, months, and years. *Time is God's invention to keep everything from happening at once*. God created time as a limited part of His creation to accommodate the workings of His purpose.

The question screaming from the amphitheater of life is this: *how is your life being branded with God's face and name on it?* Like D'Anthony—who intentionally marked his life in celebration of the ones he loved—*will the face and name of God be on your dash?!?* How is your life being stained *by* and *with* intention?

THE SIGNATURE OF THE SOVEREIGN WILL CONTINUE TO SHOW UP IN INVISIBLE INK, IF YOU REJECT THE INVITATION TO INTENTIONAL LIVING.

All of heaven is beckoning you! There is a great cloud of witnesses rooting for you! Heroes and she-roes of the faith are cheering you on! *The heart of God is literally longing for purpose and destiny to be released in you.* Decide to *rob the grave*! Accept God's invitation to *live full and die empty*! *And mark your life so that life knows you were here.*

CHAPTER 8

CONVERSATIONS WITH THE PREGNANT GRAVEYARD

The graveyard is pregnant with the unborn offspring of procrastination and eventuality! Dr. Chiffon Foster (2018) hit the nail on the head: "One of saddest moments in a person's life is not earthly death but the earthly death of one who never walked in destiny" (p. 3). Dr. William Dwight McKissic Sr., Pastor of the Cornerstone Baptist Church in Arlington, TX echoed this sadness but laced it with joy when he sermonized, "What you give is going to last; what you keep is going to be lost." Death often keeps an unscheduled itinerary in the lives of those not expecting a visit.

The graveyard is overflowing with ***unfulfilled purpose, untapped potential***, and ***unreleased possibility. The cemetery is a ready and ripe recipient to swallow up the 'nevers of life'***… the never lived, never sang, never spoken, never written, never confessed, first steps never taken, businesses never birthed, hopes never pursued, relationships never discovered or recovered, ideas never consummated, healing never claimed, recovery never apprehended.

The prophetic voice of Dr. Martin Luther King, Jr. never rang truer when he conducted the eulogy for the four young innocent victims of the 1963 bombing of Sixteenth Street Baptist Church in Birmingham, Alabama.

On September 18, 1963 he offered comfort to the bereaved families & nation. In his eulogy, Dr. King made this heartfelt proclamation to provide medicine for the moment: **"Death is the irreducible common denominator of all men"** (King, 1963, para 6). And so, we find comfort from Christianity's affirmation that death is not the end. Indeed, "Death is not a period that ends the great sentence of life, but a comma that punctuates it to more lofty significance" (King, 1963, para 7).

> NONE OF US ARE EXEMPT FROM EXPERIENCING DEATH.
> IF WE ARE NOT EXEMPT FROM DYING,
> THEN WE ARE NOT EXEMPT FROM LIVING.

We are not exempt from Living-the-Dash between ***sunrise*** *(the day we were born)* and ***sunset*** *(the day we physically die)*. Now is the time to graduate from merely existing to intentionally living! **Standing on the bridge between the now and eternity is a conscious and intentional choice:**

- the choice that will determine how *we **Live-the-Dash***;
- the choice to decide *how we live rather than how long we live*;
- the choice to determine if we are going to *count days or make days count*.

We are all confronted—whether the challenges or issues of life have **anesthetized us** from *living* or **desensitized us** to *living*—we are all arrested by the inquiry to investigate the purpose of life.

I encourage you to ponder these six questions as you read through this chapter:

1. How do I accept God's divine invitation to live *the* question of intentional living?
    - This constitutes living *into* the question as well as living *out* the question.

2. Will I accept the "quality makes quantity meaningful" ***mission statement for living***?

3. Will I choose to just *expire* or will I also choose to *inspire*?

4. ***How do I make, master, and maximize moments and divorce myself from making appointments with borrowed time?***

5. ***How can I stop being a malnourished tenant whose address is 'would of / could of / should of' boulevard?***

6. ***Since eventuality has been a calling card with ceaseless minutes in my life, how do I now embrace intentionality as a birthmark to brand my life?***

My God!! I know what it is like to *feel* stuck. I know what it is *to be* stuck. I am familiar with the desperate sighs of a heart damaged by ***canceled reservations***. I am no stranger to seasons of life riddled with ***anesthetized expectations***. *I know what it means to have inconsistency as my greatest consistency.* I know what it is like to feel trapped between ***what could be*** and *what should be* and *what is not*. I am no stranger to being *wounded by not yet* and *afflicted by defeated potential*.

I am all too familiar with *amputated hope*! With being *too scared to dream* and instead *choosing the safety of resignation*. Yes, in my life sometimes it has seemed better **not** to feel, not to want, and not to hope. *We have all been injured by the promise of possibility.* And if we are honest, you and I have at times felt like God has abandoned and forsaken us.

Be Encouraged is the name of the life-inspiring daily devotional that Dr. Ralph Douglas West offers to the global faith community. He imparted this exhortation in the March 11, 2019 devotional:

> "A moment comes when you will ask, "Where is God?!" There are some who suggest that asking that question makes you less spiritual. On the contrary, if you never ask the question, then you're probably not growing in faith. This question can only be asked by those who are familiar with the presence of God to sense His absence. There comes a time in the life of every believer when it feels like God has abandoned you. But it is when God seems the farthest from you that He is really the closest to you."

Yes, broken dreams and broken wings have a way of distorting the meaning and movement of life! The in-between spaces of wilderness, promise, and inheritance can be challenging, crippling, and confounding terrain.

Be encouraged! ***God does not want any of the stuff back that He has so graciously deposited in you.*** Let patience have its perfect work in you that you may be complete, lacking nothing (James 1:2-4). *Continue* to seek and you will find; life will open to you (Luke 11:9-10). *Failure is not your enemy*; *lack of effort* and *fractured hope* are your foes (Proverbs 24:16). You are *surrounded by a great cloud of witnesses* rooting for you (Hebrews 12:1-2). *Keep* pressing (Philippians 4:13). Keep praying (1 Thessalonians 5:17). Be steadfast because your effort *is not* in vain (1 Corinthians 15:58). *Hope* is available and accessible (Romans 15:13). **The Lord has a vested interest in your success** (Philippians 1:6).

Jackson Teller of the FX television series *Sons of Anarchy* dropped some serious knowledge when he waxed philosophically in one of the episodes. Jax proclaimed, ***"Every day is a new box. We open it and look at what's inside. You are the one who determines if it is a gift or a coffin."*** Dr. Donald L. Parson—one of the greatest thinkers and preachers of any generation—made an emphatic announcement! This announcement literally represents a declaration from the very heart and throne room of God. It speaks directly to the charge to rob the grave and move at the speed of intention. Dr. Parson declared, *"You want people to know you came when you have gone."*

GRAVE ROBBERS

The Hebrew Scriptures teach that we are unable to voice what we cannot comprehend (Ecclesiastes 1:8). It also teaches that God has placed **within us a deep seated, gripping desire to transcend our mortality** by knowing the **what** (*purpose*) and **why** (*destiny*) for living (Ecclesiastes 3:11). The Preacher in Ecclesiastes heralded that *NOTHING IS BETTER than seizing the day* (Ecclesiastes 3:12).

Mariam-Webster defines a *grave robber as "a person who digs up a buried body to steal the things that were buried with it"*. Grave robbers uncover graves or tombs or crypts to raid and rob them of valuable artifacts or personal effects. The grave of silent film icon Charlie Chaplin was opened and his entire coffin stolen. One of the sons of President William Henry Harrison was a victim of grave robbing. Some grave robbers steal the corpses after burial for medical dissection and sell organs on the black market for profit. Others steal the bodies for dissection and anatomy lessons for medical students. It has been said that grave robbers destroyed history when they emptied the Mayan Tomb before archaeologists could examine its contents.

In this book I use "grave robbers" to articulate the mandate for the living not to take anything of value to the grave. ***See yourself as a grave robber. Do not allow neglected goals, abandoned ideas, and deserted potential to be buried with you.*** I think you would agree that it would be beyond improper and perplexing for a U-Haul truck to follow the hearse to the graveyard and to your burial site!

Every day is a new box. When you open it and look at what's inside, is it a gift or is it a coffin? What's in the box???

1. Is it dead stuff that was never given life?
2. Is it ideas that suffocated due to lack of breath for your passion and imagination?
3. Is it the carcass of a book you still haven't written or a concept or idea you still haven't pursued?
4. Is it the corpse of dead stuff connected to words never spoken, decisions never made, dreams never chased, potential never released, or time never spent?
5. Is it stuff you let die due to depression or discouragement or despair?

WHAT'S IN THE BOX? GOD DESIRES IT TO BE A GIFT NOT A COFFIN? WHEN YOU LOOK INSIDE THE BOX OF THE DAY WHAT IS IT?

It is worth repeating: ***the last thing the Father of good gifts*** (see Romans 8:32; James 1:17) ***desires is for you to give heaven back unused currency.***

TALENT LESSONS: ROBBING THE GRAVE

The tragedy in the **Parable of the Talents** taught by Jesus (see Matthew 25:14-30; Luke 19:12-27) is twofold:

1) The servant buried the gift.
2) The servant said he knew better than the Master what to do with what he was given.

In this parable, two of the servants made the most of what was given to them. Scripture reveals they reproduced the currency entrusted to them (see Matthew 25:16-17, 20-23). However, the servant who was given one talent turned out to be *rebellious*, *lazy*, and *unproductive* (see Matthew 25:18, 24-27). He *rejected the responsibility*. He *misunderstood the assignment*. He also failed to realize *reward is based on faithfulness* and *not the size of the responsibility*.

Did the idle and short-sighted servant think burying the currency would produce interest? Did he think burying the talent the Master gave him would benefit from the soil surrounding it... that it would experience high yielding interest from the ground he buried it in? **Jesus is yet encouraging you not to bury or hide the currency He entrusted to you.** Of course, we should be careful not to be too hard on this servant. Like this unproductive servant in Matthew 25, you and I have also either been guilty of or are being guilty of:

- burying gifts God has given us
- resisting responsibility
- lacking follow-through
- failing to make the most of opportunities
- lacking wisdom and trafficking in disobedience
- telling God that we know better than He does with what He has given us
- ignoring the privilege and opportunity to make the most of the currency God entrusts to us

The unfaithful servant did more than mishandle and mismanage the currency. He also tried to manipulate it. One could argue the servant tried to redesign the talent and repurpose and cause it to operate in a manner that God never intended (see Matthew 25:24-25). **Bottom line: Do not bury gifts! Do not hide them! Instead, manage and multiply them.** God does not want you to give Him back unused gifts!!!

When Jesus returns to settle the accounts of life (see Matthew 25:19, 29-30) **my prayer is you are found trustworthy with the currency God has commended to your custody.** C. S. Lewis understood this prophetic and practical principle well. In the Christian classic *Mere Christianity*, Lewis

(1952) wrote, *"If you read history you will find that the Christians who did the most for the present world were just those who thought most of the next"* (p. 66). Live Full! Die Empty! *The spent life is a profitable life.* Use your abilities and gifts to serve God and others.

You cannot passively preserve or covertly participate in what God has invested in you. Do not waste opportunities like the unprofitable servant did in the Parable of the Talents. *Currency only produces interest when it is invested and/or placed in environments conducive to produce returns.* Environments matter. Soil matters just as much as Seed. Seize the day! TODAY! Make the decision to live full and die empty.

10 Life Lessons from the Parable of the Talents
1) Do Not Misunderstand the Heart of the Master.
2) Be Careful Not to Assign Your Agenda to God.
3) Be Inspired by God's Investment.
4) Be Committed to the Assignment Entrusted to You and What has been Endowed in You.
5) Be Diligent to Define Success the Way God Does.
6) In God's Economy, Responsibility isn't the Equality; Faithfulness is.
7) Be Mindful to Optimize Opportunities.
8) Accounts will be Settled by the Master. Accountability is Unavoidable.
9) God is Responsible for Success (Achievement). You are Responsible for Faithfulness (Action).

10) Embrace the Eschatology of Now. Operate Today with Eternity in Mind.

Accept God's invitation to intentional living. It is for His glory and (y)our good! Move at the speed of intention. What's in the box? Is it a womb? Or is it a tomb? Is it a gift? Or is it a coffin? You make the distinction. Make it a gift and turn tomorrow into today!

CHAPTER 9

TURN TOMORROW INTO TODAY

"Now listen, you who say, **'Today or tomorrow** we will go to this or that city, spend a year there, carry on business and make money.' Why, **you do not even know what will happen tomorrow. What is your life? You are a mist** *that appears for a little while* **and then vanishes**" (James 4:13-14, English Standard Version).

The Book of James is primarily practical rather than theoretical. The half-brother of Jesus is full of practical advice. As such, James, as the first pastor of the Jerusalem church (see Acts 12:17, 15:13; Galatians 2:1, 9-10, 12), writes as a pastor, rebuking and encouraging Christians. James stresses the importance of ***putting faith into practical action***. He encourages believers to live consistent Christian lives in the midst of persecution for our faith in Christ.

James instructs us to ***submit to God*** (James 4:7) so that we might escape the flesh (4:1-3), the world (4:4-5), and the devil (4:6-7). Wilmington's Guide to the Bible (1981) maintains that we are encouraged to do this so that "we might enjoy God's ***grace*** (see James 4:6), God's ***guidance*** (see James 4:13-15), and God's ***goodness*** (see James 4:10)" (p. 514). The Book of James' practical and pastoral tone is on full display when the Apostle declares, "for you are a *bit of smoke* that appears for a little while then vanishes" (James 4:14b, Christian Standard Bible translation). ***Faith cannot get more practical when we are encouraged to accept God's guidance regarding the shortness of our lives.***

In this passage the Apostle James calls our attention to ***the brevity of our lives.*** He counsels us on life and pleads with us to consider that life is a mist. That is, it is here and then it is gone! ***Our days on this earth are fleeting! Hence, we are urged to invest ourselves in God's work and be engaged in matters that will have eternal significance.*** The metaphor of life being a mist (vapor) reminds us that life is chased away by the morning sun. ***With the passing of each day, we are closer to the grave.*** We cannot squander the time we have been given.

I have experienced some deep emotions in the journey of writing this book. It has been a cathartic voyage. I have expressed some very personal feelings and thoughts around frustration with life and its many challenges. Namely, I have been very open about my desperation to accept God's invitation to intentional living. ***Currently I am exasperated by the fact I am still on the sideline of pastoral ministry despite no longer being on the sabbatical prompted by personal and professional renewal.***

I am facing unexpected challenges and unforeseen difficulties to secure higher education teaching (tenure track or non-tenure tack) opportunities in sacred and/or secular institutions. *My very passions and the things that bring me intrinsic satisfaction continue to elude me on many levels.* Uncertainty is swirling around me. The perfect storm of unscheduled adversity and unanticipated barriers have been banging on my door. *I am thankful for the genius and grace of God in the midst of the accidental notes of my life.* Writing has permitted me to live out loud as I seek to manifest the Master Composer's intended sound for my life. Writing has also allowed me to recalibrate my fears and faith.

AUTOPSY OF BIOGRAPHIES

This book is truly an unshielded autobiography. Typically those in public life have biographies that *depict the highlights of life without the cliff notes*. Usually the biography is a *pristine self-portrait absent pain and shame, containing photo-shopped scar tissue*. It does not articulate the seasons of fragile despair, fractured faith, and fatigued hope. Biographies read in secular conferences and church settings almost without fail do not showcase the downs, the outs, and the in-betweens. They typically *omit the almosts and the false starts*. Most often they *fail to give audience to catastrophes, broken heartedness, and regrets. Biographies predictably edit out failures, times we've missed God, occasions we blew it, and seasons we almost gave up.*

This book is not one of those public gems sanitized by a skillful publicist committed to brand management. *After all, God is significantly more interested in building His Kingdom not your brand. This work rejects a conflated Christianity infected with commercialism and consumerism.* Chapter 10 in this book serves as a prophetic and pointed critique of capitalistic systems that seek to decolonize our faith and **promote defective definitions of success**. Just because you know defeat does not make you a loser.

UNCERTAINTY AND STORMS CAN JUSTIFY INACTION IN YOUR MIND BUT STAGNATION IS TOO EXPENSIVE AND IT COSTS TOO MUCH TO STAND STILL.

I am a winner, but I know what it is to lose. I am an overcomer, but I have experienced being overcome. I am writing about intentional living, but *if you inspect the pages of this book closely you will see they have been soiled with tears, silt, and sediment from pits of despair and at times, a struggling faith.* I am penning a work about moving at the speed of intention because I have had seasons of passive existence marked by wholesale resignation. **Uncertainty and storms can justify inaction in your mind BUT stagnation is too expensive and it costs too much to stand still.**

CALLING e2I CHAMPIONS

Pastor Christopher Eugene Malone, Sr. is undoubtedly one of the greatest preachers and gifts in this generation. In the words of my beloved brother, *"You have the DNA of a champion. And champions may get knocked down but they don't stay down!"* My writing is not only an emptying; it is also a pouring. *This book is for the e2I champion in you*. (**Appendix B** highlights the **Traits of an e2I champion**). My writing is a clarion call to accept God's divine invitation to a spent life. No matter the station or season in your life, this book is committed to providing you clarity, context, content, and capital to move at the speed of intention. Whether you are:

1) *Graduating from 'saying yes' and 'doing no'* → abandoning the spirit of chronic deferment and oath breaking –or–
2) *Slowing down to speed up* → assessing motives, goals, priorities, relationships, and environments –or–
3) *Recalibrating next steps* → exploring ways to normalize and optimize excellence

my divine assignment from my Wounded Healer and Conquering King is clear. It is to…

- **Add Seasoning to Your Season**
  - **Champion the Champion in You**

- **Encourage and Equip You to Live-the-Dash**
- **Love YOU to Life!**

My prayer is you will leverage this work as a *personal, practical,* and *provoking* guide to forever end your barren relationship with procrastination and terminate your toxic agreement with eventuality.

- Move at the Speed of Intention!
- Live-the-Dash!
- Rob the Grave!
- Turn Tomorrow into Today!

REAL LIFE EXAMPLES FROM DR. P.

I had many moments where I knew I needed to write, but I permitted life to keep me from doing so. The irony is I was living this book but not writing it. ***Its ink was staining the pages of my life, but had yet to stain the pages of this manuscript.*** So, I had to schedule time during my very busy life for intention. I made conscious and deliberate decisions to confront the truth espoused by Nicole Crank (2017): ***"Sometimes we have so many things pulling for our attention that nothing actually gets our attention"*** (p. 17). There were times the scheduled intention was 1 hour a day. At other times the hour turned into hours. At other times the hour turned into a writing retreat that consumed entire weekends. At other times the hour was dwarfed to 30 minutes. And in the spirit of transparency, there were times I would go weeks without writing.

During seasons of inactivity the **conversations in my head were actively sabotaging my desire to be intentional**. These gnawing sentiments produced self-doubt and crippling opposition to progress and purpose. The thoughts went something like this *(maybe they will sound somewhat familiar to you and relate to your area[s] of inactivity)*…

- "You know it's been at least 5 days since you've written."
- "Here's another example of your saying yes and doing no."
- "Do you even know how to write a book?"
- "Who wants to hear what you have to say anyway?"
- "You're running from this because you know you don't have anything meaningful to offer."
- "How in the world are you going to write a book about being intentional and you are not consistently intentional?"
- "Your life is way too busy for this anyway."
- "How are you going to do this?"
- "You have failed too many times. Do you really want to fail again?"
- "What makes you think your voice and/or your experience even matters?"
- "Is it even worth it?"
- "Aren't you supposed to be much further along in life than you are right now?"
- "What makes you believe this is even going to matter anyway?"

In many ways my thoughts were justifying procrastination and enticing eventuality. There were several days I would end up feeling discouraged and defeated. But with God's help I was determined! ***Determination began to dwarf my doubt. Doubt was transformed to belief. Belief was transferred to expectation. Expectation transmitted to action.***

Key Principles and Lessons to Take Away from These Real Life Examples

- **Principle 1:** Turn Statements in Your Head into Questions and Become Determined to Live the Questions.
    - ✓ ***Lesson 1:*** *Re-cast Your Thoughts to Another Role in the Production of Your Life.*

- **Principle 2:** See the Value of Incremental Steps.
    - ✓ ***Lesson 2:*** *Welcome Small Steps for They are Gigantic Leaps in the Realm of Intention.*

- **Principle 3:** Make Deliberate and Conscious Decisions Today About Your Future.
  - ***Remember Your Future is Auditioning in Your Present.***
    - ✓ ***Lesson 3:*** *Be Careful Not to Allow Competing Priorities to Interrupt God's Itinerary in Your Life or Allow Busyness to Invade God's Agenda for Your Life.*

- **Principle 4:** Connect and Celebrate Moments; Make Them Meaningful.
  - *Do Not Forget, Your Present is Auditioning for Your Future.*
    - ✓ *Lesson 4: Stop Being Consumed By What You Are Not Doing and Give Sufficient Audience to What You Are Doing.*

Lesson 4 has been the most difficult in my journey to **Moving at the Speed of Intention**.

- ❖ Maybe the most challenging lesson for you are crippling thoughts **(see Principle 1)**.
- ❖ Or maybe it is getting the courage to simply take a step in the direction of your preferred future **(see Principle 2)**.
- ❖ For others your most difficult challenge is simply slowing down in order to speed up **(see Principle 3)**.

God knows each one of these lessons have been (and may even remain) present in your life. *And many times they even operate in concert; tag teaming your heart, head, hands, and feet.*

My heart, head, hands, and feet have been mostly challenged by **failing to allow what I have done and what I am doing** to energize my demonstrated commitment to the future. *Solely focusing on what I was not doing hijacked my gaze and placed me in a sunken place.* I had to learn to give sufficient audience to what I had done… to what I was (am) doing.

I learned to celebrate the victories of manifested intention. The speed of intention is not necessarily associated with velocity. ***The speed of intention is connected to purposeful activity.***

I continue to relentlessly pursue adjunct teaching positions at the university level. I intentionally prepared myself for my preferred future by obtaining a Master of Arts in Education with an emphasis in Educational Leadership (M.A.Ed.) along with a Doctor of Philosophy (Ph.D.) in Organizational Leadership. Additionally, I continue to persistently seek out seminary and Bible College teaching opportunities. I intentionally prepared myself for this by obtaining a Masters in Divinity (M.Div.) and Doctor of Ministry (D.Min.).

> IT IS NOT ABOUT THE DEGREES.
> IT IS ABOUT TO THE DEGREE IN WHICH I STRIVE TO OPERATE
> IN THE REALM OF INTENTION?

I desire to finally come off pastoral sabbatical and become active again in pastoral ministry (completed PhD in December 2014). So, I intentionally pursue relationships with church planting organizations, attend multi-ethnic church conferences, and read multi-ethnic church literature. ***My tomorrow will thank me today!*** I am at the table engaged in meaningful conversations. I am actively partnering with God to secure a chair at the tables of academia, seminary, and pastoral ministry.

Paragraphs That Changed My Life

To: Belmont University (Penned September 10, 2018)

My Christian faith is revolutionizing, informing, and influencing my personal and professional life. The unrelenting desire to live out and into my calling more fully is converging with my personal life as the love of my life is a valued and respected faculty member at Vanderbilt University. Prior to my current assignment I served as a Chief of Staff at my private defense firm's headquarters in St. Louis, MO. My company recently relocated me to Dallas, TX in support of enterprise-level synergy and integration activity across multiple businesses and sites. I enjoy my job very much. And I strive daily to bring God glory (see Eccl. 9:10; Col. 3:23). However, this is a career; not my calling. Faith that works (c.f. Jam. 2:14-26) does not live life in the discussion room forever. I want to rob the grave and depreciate its value by accepting God's divine invitation to intentional living! I desire to be part of a Christian community of learning and service passionate about equipping students for service and leadership throughout the world.

I pray my curriculum vitae (CV) and other artifacts effectively highlight my background, passions, and experience as I seek to live full and die empty and run for the applause of heaven. Thank you for your sincere consideration to join such a passionate student-centered Christian community of learning and service. Your guiding principles on the path to 2020 reflect an infectious and deliberate interplay between strategic discussion, thinking, and action in alignment with your institutional character. A Christian community and academic center of excellence like Belmont is what God had in mind for me before He formed me in my mother's womb!

To: Vanderbilt Divinity School (Email Sent October 16, 2018)

Dean Townes,

My name is Patrick Oliver and I am interested in employment and professional development opportunities at the Divinity School at Vanderbilt University. The long arc of my call has led me to pastoral ministry and supporting interfaith, interdenominational, and multi-ethnic chapel communities in the military (Air Force). I have spent the last 14 years in the private defense industry and love my job. However, this is a career; not my calling. The professoriate, in partnership with pastoral ministry, remains my ultimate goal **(my CV and Cover Letter are attached for your review)**.

I am interested in teaching (tenure track or non-tenure track) and/or research opportunities in the Divinity school. I would love to join this diverse community of inquiry on this adventure of faith and scholarship starting in Fall 2019. Such an opportunity will permit me to operate in communal spaces of intellectual curiosity and rigor stained by love, thoughtfulness, humility, and grace. Persons may differ ideologically, but that in no way should deconstruct, objectify, or dehumanize respective identities. Communities should be able to differ theologically and yet enjoy creative tension while valuing persons and perspectives.

My good friend and colleague Nicole M. Joseph (Assistant Professor of Math Education at Vanderbilt) knows of my interest in the Ph.D. in Religion at Vanderbilt. She made an E-introduction to Herbert Marbury and I sent him a follow-up note providing more detail about my interest in the program. These are four lines of inquiry I am interested in pursuing:

1. Leveraging the Hermeneutic of Suspicion to Reconstruct Interpretive, Social, Cultural, and Political Power

2. Exploring Bibliology and Textual Criticism through the Lens of Race, Class, and Culture

3. Is There a Middle Ground Between Religious Liberty, Sexual Orientation and Gender Identity Policies in Schools of Divinity Across Disparate Theologies?

4. Influence of Conscious Social Locations on the Religious Identities of Same-Sex Couples

Would you be able open to a 15 minute professional development discussion to discuss the variety of pathways to attain my professional goals?

Respectfully,
Patrick J. Oliver, Ph.D., D.Min.

Note: these engagements are only snapshots of an extremely small subset of letters and applications submitted to various academic (secular and sacred) institutions since June 2010. The Lord is inviting all of us to remain committed to living out and into what Heifetz and Linsky (2002) exclaimed:

"Give up the love they [we] know for a love they've [we've] never experienced by convincing them to take a leap of faith in themselves and in life" (p. 26).

These paragraphs changed my life because they serve as a testament of my not giving up. They have invigorated my faith when I needed it the most! They galvanize my refusal to resign! These paragraphs *function as artifacts* that I am pressing and pursuing purpose on purpose for purpose. They also serve as *sign posts and reminders I am on the path of intention*. Let's be honest: *apprehending purpose* and *being apprehended by it* are not easy. Nonetheless, I utterly refuse to be a passive participant in this journey of life. And I continue to decline the persistent invitation to throw in the towel. By faith I continue to accept God's invitation to intentional living.

The fact that you are reading this book means you have resolved to be an active partner in your preferred future. You can and must *overcome feelings of discouragement and defeat*. Conley's (2017) reassurance is timely, "*Your vision has value* and it's going to take work to get all of it to come through" (p. 81). With the Spirit's enablement, you can and must *stop justifying procrastination*. You can and will *end your relationship with eventuality*. Turn tomorrow into today! TODAY!

Let us review… these lessons will go a long way in (1) transforming doubt into belief, (2) transferring belief to expectation, and (3) turning expectation into action.

- **Lesson 1:** re-cast your thoughts to another role in the production of your life
- **Lesson 2:** welcome small steps for they are gigantic leaps in the realm of intention
- **Lesson 3:** be careful not to allow competing priorities to interrupt God's itinerary in your life or allow busyness to invade God's agenda for your life
- **Lesson 4:** stop being consumed about what you are not doing and give sufficient audience to what you are doing

Applying these lessons will move you down the path to successfully living in your dreams.

CHAPTER 10

LivINg the Dream

e2I LESSONS FROM JOSEPH THE DREAMER

A steadfast and persevering spirit is needed in order to see moments as significant and to make them meaningful. Ask God daily to increase your capacity to give these moments ample audience. Doing so emboldens commitment to the preferred and yet unfolding future. We learn this from Joseph the Dreamer! ***The life of Joseph teaches us that moving at the speed of intention is a faith walk and lifestyle.*** Joseph did not just live the dream; he lived **IN** the dream as it unfolded. Beloved, you must learn to live in your preferred future in order to live it out.

While we serve a God of suddenly (e.g. see Acts 2:1-4; John 2:7-11; Mark 1:30-31, 40-42; Matthew 8:28-32; 9:1-8, 18-26), ***the genius and providence of God often operates in delayed manifestation. And this manifestation is evolutionary and revolutionary!*** Joseph was **17 years old** when he was **sold into slavery** by his jealous brothers (see Genesis 37). He was **30 years old** when he **rose to power** in Egypt… only second in command to Pharaoh (see Genesis 41).

God was with Joseph when he:

1. was betrayed by family (see Genesis 37);

2. experienced repeated temptation at the hands of his boss's wife (see Genesis 39);
3. was slandered and falsely imprisoned (see Genesis 39) and
4. was forgotten and abandoned by those he had helped and supported (see Genesis 40).

Joseph was put in charge of nations and their resources **13 years after** the accidentals of tests, temptations, betrayals, and disappointments attempted to alter the key signature of his life. Joseph was consulted by the ruler of Egypt over a decade after he was sold into slavery.

A PROPHETIC CRITIQUE OF DEFECTIVE DEFINITIONS
OF SUCCESS IS IN ORDER.

In the Lord's Prayer (see Matthew 6:5-14, c.f. 9-14) *Jesus overwhelmingly spends more time teaching humanity about* "OUR" (verses 9, 11-12), "US" (verses 11-13) and "YOUR" (verses 9-10, 14) *that you wonder how self-centeredness* (i.e. ME, MY, I) *ever makes it into the lexicon of Christianity* or secular writings for popular press. *Jesus was not only teaching us how to pray; He was teaching us how to live. This shows up in the life of Joseph as individualism and selfish ends were never welcomed guests in the compass or composition of his life.*

GOD-SHAPED SUCCESS DOES NOT COMPROMISE THE
COMPASS OR COMPOSITION OF YOUR LIFE.

This prophetic critique of defective definitions of success examines conflated Christianity and how it has been infected with commercialism, capitalism, and consumerism. ***There are times we miss the Lord because we are so consumed with labels****. (For example – how much something costs; what color are the bottom of our shoes; what (who) are we wearing; what kind of car do we drive; how much do we make a year; what is our zip code; how many church members do we have; how many people does our sanctuaries seat; what's our annual budget; how many services and campuses do we have; etc.).* Consumerism undermines our faith because we assign value to ourselves (and others) based on such things. ***We can and will never attain the approval of these cruel spiritual masters*** (Vanderklay, 2006).

THIS IS AN IDOLATROUS TRAP UNDERWRITTEN BY THE THEOLOGIES OF ME-NESS, OTHERING, MEANING CREATION, AND IDEALIZED IDENTITY.

Just as tragically, it is not unusual for the Body of Christ to miss the glorious manifestations of God in daily living because of how we typically view signs, wonders, and speaking gifts (see Matthew 16:1-4; 1 Corinthians 12:28; Romans 12:3). ***We typically miss the plan, genius, and purpose of God.***

WE MISS IT BECAUSE WE HAVE BEEN SOCIALLY CONDITIONED TO BE IMPRESSED WITH SIZE, VOLUME, NOISE, NUMBERS, AND THE BIG SPLASH.

God was with Joseph along his journey. *Moment-by-moment, the divine fingerprint of presence and faithfulness were on display*.

1) Joseph's father [Jacob] *kept his dreams in mind* despite the jealously of his brothers (Genesis 37:11).
2) Reuben *saved Joseph's life* and *thwarted the plan* to kill him (Gen. 37:21).
3) Judah suggested they *sell Joseph instead* of taking his life (Gen. 37:26-27).
4) *Potiphar made Joseph overseer of his house* and put him in charge of all he had (Gen. 39:2-6).
5) Joseph's boss *put him in prison instead* of taking his life (Gen. 39:19-20).
6) *The warden of Potiphar's prison put Joseph in charge* of all the prisoners and all their affairs (Gen. 39:21-23).
7) The power of God allowed Joseph to *interpret the dreams of troubled souls* (Gen. 40:5-19).
8) *Joseph's faith still had vision for the future* (40:14) despite his hurtful past (40:15).
9) Those who God used Joseph to bless and restore *remembered him* (41:9-13).
10) The *ruler of Egypt* requested *Joseph the dreamer* (37:19) to interpret his dreams (41:15).
11) *God delivered Joseph out of the pit of prison* (41:14).
12) *Joseph testified of the power of God* and *refused to take credit himself* (41:16).

13) God used Joseph to interpret the ruler of Egypt's dreams (41:25-36).
14) **Pharaoh testified of the presence and wisdom of God in Joseph's life** (41:37-39).

Moment-by-moment God was with Joseph. The Lord was there during his betrayal, enticement, defamation, confinement, rejection, setbacks, regrets, and disappointment. *Joseph still had an appetite for intention.* His appetite to Live-the-Dash and Move at the Speed of Intention *did not collapse under the pressure of pain or recede due to the waves of trouble*. As the gifted voice of Pastor Joseph C. Manaway so pointedly proclaimed, "Let's be clear. Contrary to how it seems, some of us aren't stormproof. We've just learned how to dance in the rain." This was certainly Joseph the Dreamer's testimony despite the forecast. And just as importantly, *Joseph discerned the glorious manifestations of God in his life as training for reigning!* He realized his passion for intentional living *did not exempt him from seasons of delayed manifestation* on the way to his preferred future.

Joseph did not simply see his life and delayed manifestation as <u>enduring</u>; he saw them as <u>advancing</u>! *JOSEPH DEFINED SUCCESS BY SERVING, ELEVATING, ENCOURAGING, AND HELPING OTHERS*. Joseph *trusted God and was faithful to what God has invested in him*. **Hear this if you are going to learn to dance in the rain:** ISOLATION,

EXCAVATION, and TRANSFORMATION PRECEDED ELEVATION. And this elevation was *focused on having global service and impact not seeking or celebrating individual glory and achievement*.

Success at the expense of others is nothing more than overpriced failure. Be wary, valueless deposits made in the overdrawn account of non-guaranteed funds to the hollow monument of yourself will always bounce and only render faint applause to counterfeit significance. In the Christian tradition we believe that "true freedom is found in serving others" (Nichols, 2013, p. 152). The whole enterprise of success then is "not about power and authority, but service" (Nichols, 2013, p. 70). In Joseph we see how this requires a certain kind of wisdom and maturity that when realized "achieves an integration of self that conforms to the truth of the good as it is given by God" (Werpehowski, 2007, p. 67).

15) Joseph's coat of many colors given to him by his father (Gen. 37:3) was replaced with a signet ring, fine linen, a gold chain, a chariot, nationwide respect, and unquestioned authority (Gen. 41:41-44). Joseph's global influence and impact was extensive and expansive (Gen. 41:55-57).

It is not uncommon for delays to sway us towards doubt and despair. Delayed manifestation tends to trip us up as well as trip us out. *What delays are causing you dismay right now?* Right now at this very moment my preferred future remains in delayed status. **I am divorced and unmarried** (*but my heart is open to love and to being loved*). **I am not teaching at a university or seminary nor am I pastoring a local church** (*however I am pastoring pastors, leading leaders, teaching teachers, and influencing the marketplace*). *I am yet learning to marry Preparation and Progressive Manifestation! And I am learning to connect Manifestation to Incremental Actualization!* I too urge you to connect and celebrate moments. Make them meaningful!

The ink of intentional living is staining the pages of your life. Like Joseph the Dreamer, give those moments an audience in your prayers, confessions, and imagination. *Giving them audience will eject unwanted visitors who traffic in procrastination, eventuality, discouragement, and sabotaging progress.* Let the e2I champion in you give them audience and watch God arouse and activate your (1) appetite, (2) activity, and (3) expectation for intentional living.

For 13 years (between the ages of 17 and 30) Joseph remained intentional. And for two years (between the ages of 28 and 30) *Joseph had to wait for his preferred future to fully manifest. He had to wait despite the ink of intentional living that was marking his life.* Two whole years after

Joseph was put in prison by his boss (Genesis 39:20)... two whole years (Gen. 41:1) after being used by God to minister to those who had lost favor, position, and influence (Gen. 40:5-19)... two whole years after his hopeful confession and expectation to be liberated and exonerated (Gen. 40:12-15)... it was two whole years later that Pharaoh freed Joseph from the pit of prison (Gen. 41:14).

Intentional living was engraving his life and faith throughout the journey. God never abandoned Joseph. This reminds me of something Oprah Winfrey said: "Lots of people want to ride with you in the limo, but what you want is someone who will take the bus with you when the limo breaks down." ***God was with Joseph throughout the entire season of delayed manifestation.***

> MAY THE LIFE STORY OF JOSEPH REDEFINE SUCCESS FOR YOU! GOD-SHAPED SUCCESS IS DEFINED BY SERVING, ELEVATING, ENCOURAGING, AND HELPING OTHERS.

Stay encouraged! Get engaged! Get up! Press! Stay up! Immanuel is with you! (see Matthew 1:21; Matt. 8:23; Daniel 3:24-25). Like Joseph, live IN your dream.

Leverage these 8 Dream Lessons as Training for Your Reigning:

1. Moving at the Speed of Intention is a **faith walk and lifestyle**.
2. Embrace God's definition of success. **The artificial variables of individual glory and achievement always produce counterfeit results**.
3. Maintain an appetite for intention. **Trust the genius and providence of God in seasons of delayed manifestation**.
4. Remember God is with you! Moment-by-moment **God is faithful to His faithfulness**. His divine fingerprint of presence and purpose are ever present.
5. **The purpose of God has a plan. The plan of God has purpose.**
6. **God will *tailor plans* so what *He has tailored* for you *can fit you*.**
7. **Delayed manifestation is often *a dress rehearsal*** (see Gen. 39:2-6 → Gen. 39:21-23 → Gen. 41:41-43).
8. **God will let you *wear the dream*** (Gen. 37:5-10) **when the *vision wears you*** (Gen. 41:55-57).

Rob the grave and depreciate its value by accepting God's invitation to live-your-dash. Moving at the Speed of Intention *gives life to your dreams*. It transforms procrastination and eventuality into a spent life. Your destiny can and will be accelerated by the right **mentoring**, **methods**, and **ministry**. *There is victory in the process* not just the product / outcome / end goal. *There is tension between Preparation and your Level of Expectation.*

But those tension points are really sign posts on the elevation and transformation journey. Esteem the creative tension by honoring it as purposeful and pioneering. This creative tension signifies process and progress! Moving at the Speed of Intention and Living-the-Dash is an evolutionary and revolutionary existence!!! But there are costs…

CHAPTER 11

TOLLS ON THE ROAD TO MOVING AT THE SPEED OF INTENTION

It was Friday November 2, 2018. I was traveling by car from Dallas, TX to East St. Louis, IL to support the ministry launch of one of my very best friends, Pastor Christopher E. Malone Sr. Worship services for "The Ark" were going to be in full swing. I certainly did not want to miss this historic moment in kingdom expansion. I was traveling on Highway 44 West and at 5:52pm I went through a toll booth. So, I had to stop and make a payment for my passage on this toll road. ***(There are costs on the journey of intention). There are expenses incurred on the journey to purpose and destiny.*** But in Kingdom Accounting these are not expenses; they are investments. The lady in the toll booth told me it would cost $4.75. And she even told me what the payment methods were (i.e. cash or check). The Lord began to minister to me while this exchange was taking place at the toll on Highway 44.

We often miss meaningful mile markers and milestones on our journey to realized and fulfilled destiny. ***We miss them because we fail to have the currency for the passage***. Through her toll booth window this middle-aged woman even had the audacity to ask me *"where are you* headed?" and *"what is your destination?"* I told her where I was traveling. She affirmed my current heading and informed me that I was going in the right direction. The next thing she said almost made me shout "glory!" at the window. She notified me that if I was going to stay on my current course / trajectory there would be another toll way 100 miles up the road. **(Landmarks are not necessarily meant to inform us that we are where we are supposed to be; they tell us if we are headed in the right direction).** And the woman through her toll booth window—as we were completing the toll transaction—encouraged me to acquire the **both the necessary and approved currency** before I arrived at the next transition and transaction point. My God!!! *Those who know me personally know I shouted in my car and turned my vehicle into a mobile sanctuary as I offered praise to God.* ☺

Fellow travelers, we need to have relationships with folk who are fluid in the ***dialect of destiny***. We desperately need people in our lives who are not only able to speak in the ***vernacular of our present***; we need persons who are fluid in conversing in the ***language and currency of our future***. People who can either prepare or point us to milestones or mile markers that ***serve as meals suitable for our diet of intention***. God used the lady in the tool booth to give clarity and context for my present. The Lord also used her to function as a lifeline to my future *(i.e. what currency was required and* *affirmation I was traveling in the right direction)*. ***She simultaneously spoke in the vernacular of my present along with the language and currency for my future***. These are undeniable birthmarks of intentional living. My journey demanded preparation, adjustments, and accountability.

TOMBSTONE OF LOST OPPORTUNITIES

God does not want any of His stuff back! ***Death is supposed to be spent conducting an inventory of what you gave rather than what you kept.*** The love and genius of God has created a powerful symbol that will brand and mark your life. This symbol will be attached to all human kind. It will stain all our epitaphs and score the inscriptions of our graves. This brand, this mark, this stain, this powerful symbol is **THE DASH**.

- The dash between sunrise and sunset echoes an authentic and inclusive sentiment.
- It contains either a thunderous testimony or a whimpering whisper; nonetheless it will speak.

TESTIMONY OF THE DASH

The dash does not merely testify of ***how long we have lived***; it testifies ***how we have lived***. Charles A. Tidwell (1985), past Distinguished Professor of Administration and Chair of Denominational Relationships at Southwestern Baptist Theological Seminary said, ***"Quality makes quantity***

---

meaningful" (p.13). ***So, the dash is not silent! The dash speaks!*** In it is a witness of how long we have lived. But more importantly, it speaks of how we have lived. In Psalms 30:9 David asked God *"What profit is there in my death… will the dust praise You? Will it tell of Your faithfulness?"* God is inviting you to not only live these questions. His vested interest in you is beckoning you to live *into* them. ***Live-the-Dash! Now is the time to have the courage to accept God's invitation to move at the speed of intention.*** Purpose and destiny are calling you!

Your future is calling you in your present. Your present is auditioning for your future. There are **beliefs** you must **possess** if you are going to give a benediction to procrastination, complacency, accommodation, resignation, and eventuality. There are also **behaviors** you must **practice** in order to…

1) Get Out of the Could and into the Should.
2) Live in the Key of Life.
3) Successfully Settle Your Sovereign Account and be a Faithful Steward of What God has Invested in You.
4) Rob the Grave. And
5) Turn Tomorrow into Today.

CHAPTER 12

EVENTUAL TO INTENTIONAL (e2I)

ASSIMILATE THE e2I MODEL INTO YOUR LIFE'S TOOL SUITE IN SUCH A MANNER THAT IT STAINS YOUR LIFE SO THAT IT CAN SUSTAIN YOUR LIFE.

"Purpose is the original intent in which God created you… whereas destiny is where you end up based on your decisions" (Foster, 2018, p. 1). Many times the hardest step to take in being intentional is the first step. This can become even more difficult when you are invited to adopt a series of definitive steps to guide your living. This book *is not an exhortation to living your best life divorced from the counsel of God*. It is **not meant to be** a prescriptive handbook that promotes or boasts *"6 steps to successful living"* or *"10 steps to an abundant and purposeful life."*

I HAVE FAILED AS A THOUGHT LEADER AND PUBLIC THEOLOGIAN IF YOU READ THIS BOOK AND DO NOT FEEL THE NEED TO PICK UP THE AUTHORITATIVE RESOURCES OF YOUR FAITH TRADITION.

For me the authoritative resource is the Holy Bible. Hopefully *Moving at the Speed of Intention* is a companion to the canons of your tribe.

This book posits beliefs and behaviors that must be lived out and into if you want to depreciate the value of the most expensive real estate on the planet. If you want to live a spent life that impresses (honors) God, impacts (helps) community, infects (heightens) the common good, and inspires (enhances) others, then you must possess and practice this tool suite.

The **eventual to Intentional (e2I) Model** is meant to provoke and nurture intentional living. It also serves as a playbook to guide your commitment and practical wisdom to turn tomorrow into today. We have all experienced seasonal passion that lacked the seasoning (maturity) to lead to sustainable change.

The **e2I Model** is not meant to be strictly sequential as some actions may be taken simultaneously. For example, it is not uncommon to pray while one dreams and vice versa. This concurrent model also includes sizing your dream and counting the cost, watering what is planted in you, creating a culture of anticipation, elevating your thinking in order to elevate acting, and adjusting and revising plans to strengthen or improve manifestation.

It is extremely important to understand and apply the e2I Method as an iterative and continuous process. Doing so will allow you to experience its evolutionary and revolutionary nature. This approach to *living a spent life* promises to help you *turn imagination into anticipation* and *anticipation into action*.

When Jesus returns to settle the accounts of life (Matthew 25:19) you will be found faithful because you accepted His invitation to intentional living. ***Your life will no longer show up in invisible ink. It will mark the pages of history... His-story.*** My prayer is the e2I Model allows the ***currency God has commended to your custody to reap the interest of heaven on earth***. May you live full and die empty! ***No more carcasses! No more dead stuff! No more coffins!*** Only used currency! ***Seize the day... TODAY!*** Be a grave robber! ***No more appointments with borrowed time!*** Benjamin Franklin said, *"You may delay but time will not and lost time is never found again."* ***No more saying yes and doing no! No more cancelled reservations***!

Purpose is currency of the Kingdom. Give a benediction to convenience! Break the chains of procrastination for *"it is the thief of time"* (Charles Dickens). After all, *"There are only so many tomorrows!"* (Michael Landon). Procrastination is a bad habit that can have eternal effects. ***Answer the call FOR your future FROM your future by adopting its language and feasting on its diet!*** You accomplish this by ***discontinuing any and all association with accommodation, resignation, and procrastination! Adopt the e2I Model for living and terminate your illicit affair with eventuality***! Today!

LET THE CURRENCY GOD HAS ENTRUSTED TO YOUR CARE
REAP THE INTEREST OF HEAVEN ON EARTH.

THE E2I MODEL

Your tomorrow will thank you today for moving out of the eventual into the intentional! I encourage you to add the **e2I Model** to your daily life if you truly desire to live full and die empty. It will incite and inspire you to live on purpose. ***Truth is meant to touch flesh*** (see John 1:1, 14) ***and the birthmark of a God-pleasing spent life is intentional living.*** May the iterative and continuous nature of the e2I Model stain, affirm, invigorate, and elevate your life. The tool box below indicates the **beliefs** I encourage you to *embrace* and **behaviors** you should *exercise* if you want to make every day a gift rather than a coffin. It is time to open the box and see the gift of intention inside!

Tool Suite for Intentional Living

IMAGINATION
DREAMS • DESIRES • DECLARATIONS

CONTEMPLATION
ASPIRATION • PERSPIRATION

MEDITATION
SUPPLICATION • INTERCESSION

e21

ANTICIPATION
CELEBRATION • SUCCESS

MANIFESTATION
ORIENTATION • RECALIBRATION

IRRIGATION
PLANT • REAP • HARVEST

IMAGINATION

DREAMS • DESIRES • DECLARATIONS

If you have no aim then you are aimless. Aim at nothing and you will always hit it. There is almost nothing more powerful than imagination. ***Imagination is the act of forming a mental image of something not yet present and remains an unrecorded historical event because it has never been wholly perceived or received.*** Moments before her death in season 7 of HBO's hit series *Game of Thrones*, Lady Olenna Tyrell introspectively confessed to Jaimie Lannister, *"That was my prize mistake; a failure of imagination."* Learn from this confession in the screenplay of your life. Albert Einstein said, *"Your imagination is your preview of life's coming attractions."*

Do you realize that **you serve a God with an awesome imagination!?!?!** His creative ability is unmatched! One of my favorite theologians and preachers is Dr. Quenton Chad Foster. As only he can, his poetic prose captures the magnificent and unequalled imagination of God in great fashion:

> "The Lord, the one who stepped out on the wide abyss of nothingness and by the sheer essence of His presence called a moratorium on nothingness and then declared that something be the order of the day! The Lord, the One who pushed down valleys, and pulled up mountains and scooped out the seas and holds the waters in the hem of His garment.
>
> The Lord, the One who hung the sun as a golden medallion across the neck of the universe and then gave the sun a lunar looking glass called the moon for the sun to primp in at night. And then from the residue got galactic all luminaries called the stars, flung them in their silver sockets like diamond chandeliers up against the black bosom of the night sky.
>
> The Lord, the One who cause the seasons to come and go with trip-hammer regularity and He has never had to re-regulate what He's already regulated. Because of the Lord fish are still swimming, birds are still flying, fire is still burning and water is still wetting! It was the Lord, who took our dirty souls, washed it in red blood and we came out as white as snow!"

What a purposeful and creative imagination! ***And the God of the universe has a vision for your future! And He is vested in your present!*** "You are the very mind of God manifested in the earth" (Foster, 2018, p. 3).

So, give audience to your imagination. Said differently, ***give audience to 3D***… grant audience to your **D**reams (*a*spirations), **D**esires (*b*eliefs), and **D**eclarations (*c*onfessions). Give 3D to your a-b-c → give 3D to your ambitions, beliefs, and convictions. Live in your **D**reams. Live in Your **D**esires. Live in Your **D**eclarations. This is a 3D viewing! Granting this audience allows you to (re)define success **(see Chapter 10)**.

You are a historical event waiting to be recorded. ***Imagine going to the movies and seeing your life on screen. Intentional Living is starring in the main role.*** The Holy Spirit is the Director (giving direction to the cast and crew to capture His creative vision for your life). And Jesus Christ is the Producer (managing the finances [payments], production, marketing [promotion], and distribution). **Your imagination may get you into trouble** *(ask Joseph the dreamer!)*. **But just know your imagination will always get you out of trouble** *(ask Joseph the dreamer!)*. Give yourself permission to dream despite disappointment, fear of failure, and even when it hurts to hope **(see Chapters 8, 9, and 3)**. Give audience to your dreams, desires, and declarations. Give your dreams audience so God can give it audience.

WHEN YOU GIVE AUDIENCE TO YOUR DREAMS,
YOUR DESTINY WILL GIVE YOU AN AUDIENCE.

MEDITATION

SUPPLICATION • INTERCESSION

Prayer unlocks the power of God-given imagination. *Give audience to your imagination by praying and meditating for God's guidance, will, courage, strength, protection, and favor.*

- **Supplication** is when you pray for yourself (see 1 Timothy 2:1; Psalm 4:1; 5:8; 6:4; John 17:4-5; Luke 22:42; Philippians 4:6). The enemy will try to use your heart against you. When your distribution center is in the wrong location, dispensing is expensive. Ask God to keep you centered in His will.

- **Intercession** is when you pray for someone else (see Daniel 9; 1 Samuel 12:23; John 17:15-19; Acts 12:5; Romans 8:34; 15:30; Colossians 4:2-3). This is important because kingdom partnership is of primary importance. "Surround yourself with people who support your vision and help you bring it to life" (Conley, 2017, p. 83). Welcome healthy partnerships that love and lift you. Desire relationships that stimulate and stretch you. God will send and surround you with wise counsel.

When you give audience to your God-honoring imagination in prayer and meditation, you are reflecting on His will for your life. ***The will of God for your life is of crucial significance and is the chief aim of your existence*** (see Matthew 6:10; Philippians 3:8-10; Acts 17:28; Psalm 143:10). It is good to make plans if you leave room for God to change them. ***Do not allow good things to crowd out God's best for you.*** The purposes of God takes precedence over your plans. "In his heart a man plans his course, but the Lord determines his steps" (Proverbs 16:9). ***Discerning God's will for your life includes***:

    (1) ***confirming with counsel and advisers*** (Proverbs 15:22; 11:14) and
    (2) ***surrendering to inner peace for it is the fruit of following His will*** (Philippians 4:7; Proverbs 3:5-6).

It would do your imagination well to read *Destiny Decoded* by Dr. Chiffon Foster. In this extremely powerful book she unpacks the necessity and significance of ***coaches and mentors*** (chapter 3) as well distinguishes between the roles of *travel agents, tour guides, and destiny helpers* (chapter 4) in your life. *In your meditation and reflection, you will detect what you have been infected with.*

Tʜɪs Iɴғᴇᴄᴛɪᴏɴ ɪs Dᴇᴛᴇᴄᴛᴇᴅ ɪɴ Yᴏᴜʀ
Rᴇᴄᴜʀʀɪɴɢ Dʀᴇᴀᴍs, Pᴀssɪᴏɴs, ᴀɴᴅ Iᴅᴇᴀs
(see Hebrews 1:1-2; 1 Peter 4:10; Psalm 37:4-5).

You know it is of God when…

1) **it is bigger than** *you (can't do it alone or in isolation)*
2) **it is not solely for your good** *(it benefits others; success is never individualistic),* and
3) **it glorifies God** *(draws you closer to Him, deepens your relationship).*

Discover and/or Recover what God has invested in you. God has a vested interest in your success **(see Chapter 1 in this book)**. And God is the One who defines success **(see Chapter 10)**! Please do not forget that *people are not your measure so stop comparing yourself to them* (see 2 Corinthians 10:12). Remember "the only person we compare ourselves to is who we were yesterday" (Conley, 2017, p. 84).

CONTEMPLATION

If you are going to be intentional you must consider your dreams, desires, and declarations **WITH CONTINUED ATTENTION**. View your aspirations, beliefs, and confessions as *achievable and as an expected end*. *Do you not see yourself as a grasshopper in your own sight* (see Numbers 13:33).

IMAGINATION DOES NOT ELIMINATE OBSTACLES, BUT IT DIMINISHES HOW YOU EXPERIENCE THEM.

Imagination diminishes how you perceive and tackle obstacles. The little shepherd boy David will testify to that! In 1 Samuel chapter 17 the height of Goliath is mentioned in cubits. We learn in verse 4 that Goliath was six cubits (this made him almost 10 feet tall). *Goliath's height and other intimidating dimensions* (see 1 Samuel 17:4-7) **mattered to everyone else except David** (see 1 Samuel 17:24, 25).

Goliath's dimensions did not matter to David because he viewed Goliath *through* the lens of *"the living God"* (1 Samuel 17:26). **Such a perspective diminished how he perceived Goliath!** David was not intimidated by Goliath because of his imagination. His imagination was sourced in his God-given purpose. David's identity excited (and ignited) his imagination. *Identity* (connected to "the living God") → *Purpose* (slay giants) → *Imagination* (imagined what it would be like to take down the giant by the power of God).

Contemplate your aspirations, beliefs, and confessions as doable. Then trust and actively partner with "the living God" to do it! Sweat and effort are permanent companions to fulfilled purpose. "You can't just dream about success, at some point, you must wake up and live it" (Conley, 2017, p. 72). Contemplate your recurring dreams, passions, and ideas. *They are not going to leave you alone so do not leave them alone.*

If you are going to be intentional you must: 1. *Count the Cost* and 2. *Size Your Dream*.

1) **Count the Cost**: God makes this clear… whatever you desire to do you must *sit down and count the cost and consider whether you have*

enough to complete it (see Luke 14:28). Aspiration (ambition) void of perspiration (action) is barren hope. Life is full of the bleached bones of carcasses whose autopsy reveals hollow procrastination, crippled ambition, sterile promises, and unfulfilled plans. Action without planning is unwise and guarantees failure for it is "the plans of the diligent that lead to success" (Proverbs 21:5).

You should love both the promise and gift of possibility, but you must also have an affinity for the life it is (1) calling you to and ***(2) expecting of you.*** You must count the cost. That is, ***you must recognize and agree to some terms first***. According to the infectious servant-leadership of Conley (2017), "The vision of expectations must be established" (p. 75). But beware, following your dreams, passions, and ideas will mean losing relationships with convenience, complacency, procrastination, and resignation. ***You cannot follow intention and eventuality at the same time.*** They are ALWAYS at ENMITY with each other.

Be advised: being intentional may more than likely also mean losing relationships with people, systems, or environments in your present that cannot (a) speak to your future, (b) speak from your future, and who are unable to (c) provide a diet (1) for your future (2) from your future. ***Failing to count the cost is like "a wine taster's union choosing a judge with no taste*** *buds"* (Montgomery, 1969, p. 15). ***You must count the cost if you are going to successfully disciple your dreams***.

In Proverbs chapter 6 the Lord provides **lessons He wants you to learn from the ant**.

- **Lesson 1** (Prov. 6:8): Prepare and practice for your tomorrow today.
- **Lesson 2** (Prov. 6:9): Arise from sleep walking through life. How long are you going to lie there in complacency, comfort, convenience, laziness, sameness, resignation, and inaction?
- **Lesson 3** (Prov. 6:11): Failing to be intentional will keep you in poverty. ***That is, like an armed robber, procrastination and a posture of eventuality will continue to strip your life of meaningfulness and deprive you of joy and success***.

If you are going to be intentional you must also:

2) **Size Your Dream:** Embrace the big picture and do not forget **God is bigger than your dreams**. Pastor Bryan Carter of the Concord Baptist Church in Dallas, TX encourages you to remember *"the path to success is not giant steps, but intentional small steps."* Again, *resist comparing yourself to others* (they are not your measure). It is also important for you to *stop holding yourself in contempt for the stage and status of your life*.

We learn from Adam and Eve that **falls happen! What falls forfeit, God redeems!** Apart from Christ you can do nothing (see John 15:5) but through Him you can do all things (see Philippians 4:13). Dream big for the glory of God for there is a God-sized dream inside of you. And God is ready to turn your tomorrow into today. Give yourself permission to not only see success; have the audacity (and believe God for the capacity) to agree with Him to seize it.

Sizing your dream is not only about **assessing your faith** in relation to your dream – thereby *increasing your competency level*. Sizing your dream is also about **increasing your faith** to match your dream – thus, *enlarging your commitment level*. This is part of the cost.

> GOD NOT ONLY SHAPES DREAMS, HE SHAPES THE DREAMER.
> SIZING AND PURSUING DREAMS WILL CHANGE YOU.
> (see Jeremiah 29:11; Proverbs 15:22).

Pruning is inherent in the promise and process (see John 15:1-5; John 3:30; Romans 12:12).

Take heed, when sizing your dream—whether spiritual, psychological, emotional, mental, financial, or physical in nature—this often demands having the wisdom and grit to embrace incremental steps. Have holy ambition and dream big. You were made for this! Pursuing your dreams provides opportunities to give God glory when He makes them happen.

Remember intention not only *has its own diet*; it *has its own language.* **Intentional living requires nourishment for marathons not sprints.** As you size your dream, be watchful of persons and places who **speak the dialect of procrastination, accommodation, and convenience.** Language shapes thought and thought shapes action **or** inaction. People and atmospheres who traffic in procrastination, accommodation, sameness, complacency, and eventuality **will not see** and **cannot support the vision of your life**.

IRRIGATION

PLANT • REAP • HARVEST

Water what is planted in you. And water what you plant. Feed both your faith and resolve to be in relationships and environments that speak to your future from your future.

Irrigation also entails **conducting maintenance on your commitment, insecurities, fears, doubts, and relationships.** Feeding your faith and fortitude will lead you to feast on the diet of intention. "What happens NEXT is determined by what you are eating NOW" (Foster, 2018, p. 36). **Nourishing what has been planted in you is an ongoing and iterative process. Repeated watering causes the harvest to grow deeper and fuller.** Irrigation not only helps what is in you to blossom; it also helps it to stand.

Irrigation influences root growth, plant growth, regrowth, yield, and quality. Water gives what is planted in you nutrients to grow more pastures and crops. Irrigation also aids what is invested in you to lengthen its growing season ***even during unseasonal production*** (see Genesis 8:2; Jeremiah 5:24). Remain diligent. Continue to work towards the preferred future God has planted inside you. Irrigation is an ongoing and iterative process. Repeated watering causes the harvest to grow deeper and fuller.

Keep Irrigating the God-Shaped and
God-Sized Seeds that Have Been Planted in You.

Keep watering! And remember, healthy environments and relationships matter greatly. The greatness of the God-sized and God-shaped ideas inside of you require loving, effective, agile, and intentional irrigation systems. Trust and actively partner with God to… Plant. Reap. Harvest.

ANTICIPATION

CELEBRATION • SUCCESS

What is the use of **Imagination** (*granting audience to your dreams*), **Meditation** (*praying for the will, way, wisdom, power, provision, and protection of God*), **Contemplation** (*giving continued attention and focus to your God-sized and God-honoring recurring dreams, passions, and ideas*) and **Irrigation** (*watering what's planted in you and what you're replanting*) if you fail to *expect the expected* and *celebrate manifestations of intention*?

Create a culture of anticipation. Do so unlike the church that was praying for Peter in Acts chapter 12 (see verses 5 and 12). It is always tragic for there to be a culture of participation void of anticipation **(see Chapter 4 in this book)**. God answered this praying church's petition for Peter's release from prison (see Acts 12:6-11), but they did not expect the expected (see Acts 12:13-15). Catch this – *they failed to prepare for the preferred future they* *were believing God for* (see Acts 12:16-17). *Let that marinate.* **Do not move on yet**. Let that marinate some more. Read that sentence again – <u>they failed to prepare for the very thing they were believing God for</u>. True reformation will invade your life when you learn to *live in the future tense even if* (when) *the present is tense*. This is where the purpose, power, and pull of intention is so paramount.

A wonderful example of this is on full display in Joshua chapter 6 when the city of Jericho was conquered! Joshua and the Children of Israel learned that intentional living conditions you to *rehearse readiness* (Celebration, Meditation, Contemplation, and Irrigation) as well as to *rehearse realization* (Manifestation). They walked this out! They conquered the promise land with footsteps. So, do what Pastor James Lowe of the Bethel World Outreach Church in Nashville, TN said about Joshua and the Children of Israel. "Participate in your victory!" *Expect the expected by practicing and preparing for your preferred future.* It is in this anticipation that God is conditioning you to trust Him and to celebrate manifestation.

Although we serve a God of *"suddenly/immediately"* (see Acts 2:1-4; Mark 1:40-45; Luke 7:11-17; 8:52-56; 17:11-19; John 11), life has taught you that **He is also a God of gradual manifestation** (see 2 Kings 5:10-14; Mark 8:22-25; Acts 9:1-19; Daniel 10:7-13; Joshua 6). Joseph never stopped anticipating even during his seasons of delayed and incremental manifestation (see Genesis chapters 37 and 39 – 41). ***Trust God to strengthen you to overcome disappointment when "suddenly" is not in His will*** (see Genesis 40:23; Philippians 4:6-7; Romans 8:28; Psalm 121:1-8; Isaiah 40:28-31; Psalm 73; 46:1-11; 27:1-4; 42:11; 1 Pet. 5:6-7, 10-11; Prov. 23:17-18; Psalm 34:17-18; Isaiah 41:10-16).

HOPE IS THE CURRENCY WE MUST OPERATE IN WHEN
THINGS HAVE YET TO PAY OFF
(see Hebrews 11:1; Romans 5:2-5; Psalm 71:5, 14).

Charles Haddon Spurgeon encourages you "to trust God's heart even when you cannot trace His hand." This is crucial in life, especially in seasons of delayed manifestation. Have faith in God to do what He has promised (see Isaiah 55:11; Mark 7:37) even in times of disappointment produced by delay. "God is too good to be unkind and He is too wise to be mistaken" (Charles Haddon Spurgeon). ***Give yourself permission to celebrate***. Celebrate what God has done. Celebrate His faithfulness. Celebrate the hope that is in you even if it is on life support! The God of the universe has not forgotten about you (Hebrews 6:10).

Celebrate your small victories! This fuels and refuels you and sets you in position to cross the next valley that you must cross. Or the next mountain you need to climb. Stop being consumed with what you are not doing and give sufficient audience to what you are doing. ***Learn to practice what I call 'pause for applause' moments***. Erect them. Memorialize them.

The fact that you are reading this book is a 'pause for applause' moment. The fact you have not thrown in the towel is a 'pause for applause' moment. You did not give in or give up. You kept (keep) pressing even when you do not feel like it. You kept (keep) hoping even **when it hurt to hope**. You have kept pushing and believing even when everything around you did not look like what you hoped or expected. You keep pushing when everything around you serves as a reminder of bad choices or failed decisions you made. ***You keep hoping and pressing despite things around you not looking like what you know is in you and/or what God said to you.*** Despite it all, you are still breathing!

> GIVE YOURSELF PERMISSION TO CELEBRATE.
> PRACTICE PAUSE FOR APPLAUSE MOMENTS.
> MEMORIALIZE THEM. THIS IS SOUL CARE!

You have had the audacity to keep trusting God to grant you the strength to embody the encouragement from one of the shining lights in Christianity today. You have worn this humble and faithful servant's encouragement like "a garment of praise" (Isaiah 61:3). My little brother and biblical exposition all-star Pastor Joseph C. Manaway has testified and rejoiced with you because ***you have "learned how to dance in the rain!"***

You have known failure, frustration, defeat, (borderline) depression, and heartbreak. You have experienced betrayal, unfulfillment, shame, abandonment, uncertainty, embarrassment, disappointment, crippling regret, and being misunderstood. Yet you are still here! ***Celebrate that you are still hoping. Still pressing. Still open to trying. Still believing. Still dreaming. Still planning. Still fighting. Still longing. Still living. Still dancing. Still taking steps.***

I am going to rehearse this in your hearing until it arrests you. In Jesus Name, learn to 'practice pause for applause' moments. Depend on the Spirit to empower you. And rest in the grace of Christ to comfort and compel you. In a consistent, meaningful, and sustainable way, you must learn that ***operating in the realm of intention demands covenant between your conduct and confession.*** So, connect and celebrate moments. Doing so makes them meaningful. Let them marinate! It is vitally important you ***give yourself permission*** to celebrate! ***This is soul care!!!***

You have survived. You are surviving and thriving. Celebrate! ***You are a pause for applause MOVEMENT.*** You are in the self-ship hall of fame. Plant a flag and be arrested by your healing and recovery. Celebrate you have not forgotten Who has brought you! Celebrate Who has sustained and preserved you! Celebrate that you have been kept! Selah. ***Celebrate the fact you do not suffer from spiritual amnesia!***

Your successes are sustainable! Your victories are repeatable! Your almosts are attainable! Your fears are faxable! Your wounds are reversible and curable! Your regrets can be retired! Your failures are being rewritten! Your pain is being repurposed! Your passion can be revived! Your not-yets are within your grasp! RSVP to your tomorrow, today! Amen. Yes God! With confidence and hope, make it so. God's truth must stand.

The love, grace, and strength of God have been and remain ever-present in your life. God was *with* **Joseph** (Genesis 39:2). God was *with* **Abraham** (Genesis 12:1-3). God was *with* **Moses** (Exodus 33:11; Joshua 1:17). God was *with* **Joshua** (Joshua 1:5-7). God was *with* **David** (1 Samuel 18:28). God was *with* **Solomon** (2 Chronicles 1:1). God was *with* **Hezekiah** (2 Kings 18:7). God was *with* **Daniel** (Daniel 6:19-23). ***GOD IS WITH YOU*** (Matthew 1:21; 28:20; Galatians 2:20; Romans 8:38-39; 1 Chronicles 22:17-19; Psalm 34:15; Isaiah 41:10). ***Give yourself permission to celebrate!*** Today! And know your best days are ahead of you, today! ***Do not make an appointment to celebrate.*** Procrastination is not your friend. And eventuality is your enemy. ***Celebration is wind for your win!***

HALL OF FAME

Some institutions exist to honor the acts and achievements as well as preserve the history of individuals in an activity or field. These institutions are called the *"Hall of Fame."* The Bible has its own Hall of Fame. It is found in the 11th chapter of the Book of Hebrews. It chronicles and commemorates the renowned achievements of *people of great faith*. Namely, **Abel** (verse 4), **Enoch** (verse 5), **Noah** (verse 7), **Abraham** (verses 8, 17-19), **Sarah** (verse 11), **Isaac** (verse 20), **Jacob** (verse 21), **Joseph** (verse 22), **Moses** (verses 23-28), **the Children of Israel** (verse 29 {Red Sea} | verse 30 {Jericho}), **Rahab** (verse 31), and **Gideon / Barak / Samson / Jephthah / David / Samuel** (verses 32-38). This "Hall of Fame" chapter in Christian Scripture could be problematic for the faith or perspective of those infected with commercialism, capitalism, and consumerism.

Be wary and suspicious of deformed and defective definitions of success (see Chapter 10 in this book for that prophetic critique). Yes, **1). God is a God of suddenly and immediately** (e.g. as seen at Pentecost and in the lives of the man with leprosy and the widow's son healed by Jesus). Yes, **2). God is also a God of gradual manifestation** (e.g. as seen in the life of Joseph and Joshua). However, Hebrews chapter 11 reveals He is also a **3). *God of prophetic fulfillment*.** That is, ***He is a God who manifests things in*** *eternity*. This is troublesome for Christians and non-Christians alike who hold to and lift up distorted definitions of success.

> SUCCESS IS NOT ALWAYS DEFINED BY EVENTS BEFORE YOU DIE. SOME THINGS ARE NOT SEEN, EXPERIENCED, OR POSSESSED DURING YOUR LIFETIME.

What do you do when promise has not manifested in your lifetime? Some in the Bible's Hall of Fame *"died in the faith without receiving the promise"* (Hebrews 11:13, 39). This does not make God a liar nor their faith in vain. **They are in the hall of fame of faith so one could quickly** (and erroneously) **assume their faith produced humanity's definition of earthly success**. However, when you consider success through a godly and eternal lens you know **success was bigger than what they accomplished.**

They defined and saw success in terms of the **permanency of the prize** and the **applause of heaven** over against the approval and adulation of men. For them the promise was the Person and His eternal kingdom. The promise was the future fulfillment that God would provide salvation through the perfect sacrifice of Christ; the door to a better country – heaven, the city of God (see Hebrews 11:15-16).

They died in the faith, but not without faith. Their accounts were settled by God in eternity based on the completed work of the Messiah on their behalf. ***They remained steadfast through trials and difficulty and died in the faith without having yet received the redemptive transaction of promise***. The promised-One (Jesus) has come so you have much more reason to hold on to faith and not let discouragement or tough times defeat you. The heroes and she-roes in this Hall of Fame looked forward to Jesus and His work; you (we) view it from behind and possess and delight in the fruit of His work.

God gave them promises, but they were not allowed to see their fulfillment. The promise was made to them while the fulfillment chiefly belongs to (all of) us. ***Do not relapse even when you experience fiery trials and frustrated faith or fatigued hope.*** There is a promise of future blessings. Persevere! ***This promise is purposeful for it is meant to enable and sustain us in times of trial, temptation, and persecution***.

The lives of faith of those who died in the faith without receiving the promise are meant to inspire and encourage us. These "great cloud of witnesses" (Hebrews 12:1) paved the way for us and are cheering us on to receive the like-minded victory of faith they obtained. A great many have gone before us, each bearing witness to a life of faith whose ***primary intention was*** (1) ***possessing eternal success***, not being intoxicated with (2) ***producing earthly success*** or being (3) ***possessed by it***.

Change your definitions of success and view it from an eternal lens. Maintain faith in God despite the lack of manifestation during your lifetime. Sustain a sense of faith in the surety of His goodness. Do not alter your faith in God or knowledge of Him because things may not happen when or how you want. ***God may have already provided something better for you in eternity.***

> Hebrews 11:39-40 "³⁹All these people earned a good reputation because of their faith, yet none of them received all that God had promised. ⁴⁰For God had something better in mind for us, so that they would not reach perfection without us" (New Living Translation of the Bible).

The explanatory notes of Albert Barnes restates verse 40 in Hebrews chapter 11 in this manner: "God having provided, or determined on giving some better thing than any of them realized, and which we are now permitted to enjoy." This enjoyment will be ***consummated in future glory with receipt of all its privileges and advantages.***

> "Whatever our religion may have cost us, we shall not feel that we began to serve God too early, or served him too faithfully. **Whatever pleasure, gain, or splendid prospects we gave up** in order to become Christians, we shall feel that it was the way of wisdom, and shall rejoice that we were able to do it. **Whatever sacrifices, trials, persecution, and pain, we may meet with,** we shall feel that there has been more than a

compensation in the consolations of religion, and in the hope of heaven, and that by every sacrifice **we have been the gainers. When we reach heaven, we shall see that we have not endured one pain too much**, and that through whatever trials we may have passed, **the result is worth all which it has cost**. Strengthened then in our trials by the **remembrance of what faith has done in times that are past**; recalling the example of those who through faith and patience have inherited the promises, let us go cheerfully on our way. **Soon the journey of trials will be ended, and soon what are now objects of faith will become objects of fruition, and in their enjoyment, how trifling and brief will seem all the sorrows of our pilgrimage below!**" (Barnes' Notes, Albert Barnes Bible Commentary)

God is a God enough to make things happen suddenly. He is God (and good) like that. **He is also God enough to manufacture gradual manifestation.** He is God (and gracious) like that. **And yes, God is a God enough to manifest things in eternity.** He is God (and glorious) like that. He knows all things at once and completely and simultaneously. So, *change your definitions of success and view it through an eternal prism.* Do not lose faith in or focus on the primary intention which is *possessing eternal success*. Resist being intoxicated with pursuing or producing earthly success.

Refrain from being possessed by the cadence and offspring of living in an individualistic and capitalistic society. *Its offspring of* (1) **achievement,** (2) **applause,** (3) **approval,** (4) **acceptance,** (5) **status,** (6)

power, and (7) **influence** are *attractive counterfeits that feed our fallen nature.* They pull us away from God and create distance and conflict in our fellowship with Him and each other. *May the God of promise continually deliver you from the carnal trappings of earthly success.*

I pray you allow Christ to be your *mediator* (1 Timothy 2:5), *model* (John 2:13-17; 13:1-5), and *mentor* (Luke 12:15-21; John 8:1-8; Luke 17:11-19) on your intentional living journey. *Immediate satisfaction is always found wanting on the scale of eternal value and significance. Be mindful of the 'great exchange' taught by Christ*, "And what do you benefit if you gain the whole world but lose your own soul? Is anything worth more than your soul?" (Matthew 16:26, New Living Translation of the Bible). Your soul is of higher value than all the riches and enjoyments of the world.

Do not lose heart when things do not manifest in your timing. Your definition of earthly success may not manifest during your lifetime. The plans and purposes of God take precedence over your plans. Remember the birthmarks of God-shaped plans: **(1) It is bigger than *you*** *(can't do it alone or in isolation),* **(2) It is not solely for your good** *(it benefits others so its horizontal impact can never be voided or avoided; success is never individualistic),* and **(3) It glorifies God** *(draws you closer to Him, deepens* *your vertical relationship)*. **God has already provided something better for you in eternity.**

Do not grow weary in the work. John Piper (1983) summarized it greatly, "The worst enemy of enthusiasm is time." So the Bible encourages us "not [to] get tired of doing what is good. At just the right time we will reap a harvest of blessing if we don't give up" (Galatians 6:9, New Living Translation of the Bible). God is faithful to His faithfulness. ***Celebration is wind for your expected end!***

MANIFESTATION

The process of imagination, meditation, irrigation, and anticipation *orients* your commitment and *capacity* to move from the eventual to the intentional. Capacity is defined as "the depth, width, and height of who you are" (Foster, 2018, p. 48). Capacity designates what and how much you can hold. ***ORIENTATION*** is the process you go through in which you are introduced to performance standards, policies, hours of operation, benefits, facilities, and responsibilities. ***The intent of orientation is to facilitate the adjustment or alignment of your identity with your dreams/ideas/goals to surroundings or circumstances.*** #iDig

ORIENTATION does at least 8 things. It...

1) Encourages confidence in God (***see Goliaths through the eyes of the living God***);

2) Provokes potential (***speaks to your future from your future***);

3) ***Further defines and clarifies goals and expectations*** (including the conversion of unacceptable beliefs and/or behaviors);

4) ***Acclimates you to your preferred future*** (mindsets & motives marinate the next season);

5) Calibrates the ***culture of anticipation*** to fit the ***culture of planned participation***. Plainly put, ***orientation connects you to 'similar others' and sets you up for success***.

6) ***Promotes communication*** (upward {Savior}, inward {self}, and outward {sponsors});

7) Prepares your capacity. That is, it ***marries you to commitment***.

8) Improves sustained excellence (***elevates thinking to elevated acting***).

You have to orient yourself to your future. Do not lack preparation or walk in unbelief. So many of us have mishandled and mismanaged destiny because we were not ready to receive and steward its manifestation.

THE POWER OF RECALIBRATION

RECALIBRATION is defined as "to change the way you do or think about something." ***Living intentionally demands the ability to look back while moving forward.*** There are always opportunities to recalibrate ***(adjust, refine, realign)*** things to improve the quality of your life. You must be "willing to evolve" (Conley, 2017, p. 18). This is vital if you are not going to let complacency sneak up on you or take residence in you. ***God-honoring***

success requires sustained focus. It also requires the capacity to face and acknowledge your mistakes, failures, and ineffective habits.

In his powerful book *Lead with Love*, Spencer Conley's treatment on preparation is worthy of your reflection. Conley (2017) emphatically noted, "We must be brave enough to be honest and open about getting better in our frail areas... When we do that our frail areas become strengths" (p. 7). It takes courage to confront unproductive perspectives and practices. It takes healthy self-awareness and humility to admit failure. This is why recalibration is so vital in your e2I journey.

Reflection and renewal operate in concert. They are joined at the hip and are two sides of the same coin. ***Reflection provides actionable feedback to your ongoing development.*** It highlights strengths as well as areas of improvement. Welcome the possibility you may need to recalibrate your expectations or strategy for living. ***Change and betterment only happens when you are clear about what you desire to be changed or improved.***

You are always in the state of becom*ing*. So use and sharpen your tools. ***In this life you never arrive at the point where growth is no longer necessary.*** "Honesty allows growth" (Conley, 2017, p. 102). If you are not growing, you are decaying. It is natural for eagles to shed feathers and for snakes, lizards, and even human beings to shed skin. ***Renewal is required if you are going to grow.***

> YOU WILL NOT BE ABLE TO CONVERT THE EVENTUAL INTO THE INTENTIONAL IF REFLECTION AND RENEWABLE FAIL TO BE CONSTANT COMPANIONS IN YOUR LIFE.

This growth and renewal profile includes enlarging your capacity to resist resignation, stagnation, and complacency (see 1 Peter 3:18; 2 Peter 1:5-11). It is imperative that you maintain an appetite for growth, development, and improvement.

Recalibration must be a way of life if you are going to successfully live-the-dash and be an e2I champion. You will not be able to convert the eventual into the intentional and depreciate the value of the cemetery if reflection and renewal fail to be constant companions in your life. The healthy practice of effectively looking back while moving forward will transform tomorrow, today.

Dr. Christy L. Erving, Assistant Professor of Sociology in the Department of Sociology at Vanderbilt University is right: ***"Reconciliation has to happen before continuation."*** With utter dependence on the Spirit, be open to the necessity of adjusting your goals, plans, and execution. In order to move forward while looking back, you may need to ***consider stopping doing some things altogether***. There is also the very real possibility that you need to *discover ways to repeat or increase what you are doing right!* I call this principle *"giving value to your value"*. Recalibration could mandate replication. Trust the Holy Spirit for discernment. Look back to see what you could do (i) **better** or (ii) **different** or (iii) **again**. Give value to your value!

Utilize people for wise counsel that you trust and who believe in you. "Seek expert counsel before giving up" (Conley, 2017, p. 77). *Sometimes they can see what you cannot discern.* Continuous improvement and evolution produces the necessity to adjust and refine thinking and acting. This is unavoidable because iteration induces the opportunity for revision. So, bring things into alignment with your future.

- *If it is not compatible with your God-shaped future, then stop doing it in your present.*
    - ✓ *Recalibrate!*
- *If the attitude, behavior, or action is congruent with your God-shaped future then do more of it. And do it better.*
    - ✓ *Recalibrate!*

CHAPTER 13

EPILOGUE

Thank for your reading this book. In writing it, I have learned and grown so much. I confessed earlier that its ink was staining the pages of my life while I was penning the manuscript. I am not the same man who started this book. To quote my friend and multiethnic life and ministry mentor Dr. Derwin L. Gray, the "ever-present gospel reality" has transformed me personally. It has ***deepened my passion to honor the creative, redemptive, and purposeful genius of God.* More than ever, I believe the chief end and high watermark of life rests at the foot of the cross of Christ** (see Ephesians 3:14-21; 2 Cor. 5:21; Colossians 2:14-15).

> "But with man's fall into sin, fellowship with God is broken, relationships with others are strained, work seems to always be frustrating, and man struggles to maintain any semblance of dominion over nature. *Only by restoring fellowship with God, through faith in Jesus Christ,* ***can purpose in life be rediscovered***" (GotQuestions.org, 2009).

Identity and purpose are clarified and reconciled at the cross of Christ (see Romans 5:10; John 10:10). We learn from Adam and Eve that falls happen. Learn to rehearse this reminder: **what falls forfeit, God redeems** (see Genesis 3:15; Romans 8:18). This reminder will transform your life!

The chief *end* of our existence is to glorify God and enjoy Him forever (see Ecclesiastes 12:13-14; 1 Corinthians 10:31; Romans 11:36; Isaiah 43:7; Psalm 73:24-26; John 17:22, 24). The "end" has dual function and meaning. That is, (1) our **final destination** (in heaven where we will glorify and enjoy the Lord forever) influences (2) **purposeful action** (in this present life where we strive to glorify and enjoy God and all His creation). Said differently:

- ❖ our *vertical relationship* with God has secured the blessed hope of our eternal future which subsequently
- ❖ is designed to infect and fuel all the *present horizontal dimensions* of life

Purposeful living is not possible and will "forever beckon but will forever elude" (Benjamin Elijah Mays) if you fail to accept God's invitation to intentional living. **Purpose cannot be fulfilled apart from God.**

A BETTER VISION OF YOURSELF IS REQUIRED TO BECOME
A BETTER VERSION OF YOURSELF.

To know Him is to love Him. The more you know Him, the more you love Him (see John 17:3; 1 John 4:8, 16). **The more you love God, the better you understand who you are** (identity) **and what your** (universal & individual) **purpose** in life is (see Ephesians 3:17-20; Psalm 57:2). Life (at its best) is a Christ-centered endeavor. Purpose, fulfillment and satisfaction are either discovered or recovered in the heart and mind of God (see Psalm 119:105;

James 1:5). **Purpose rediscovered then becomes purpose reimagined!** You can look for purpose and fulfillment in vain pursuits, but they will leave you with the feeling of emptiness (see Ecclesiastes 1:2).

RSVP to God's invitation. **He has sent a self-addressed stamped envelope with sufficient postage to mail it back.** The postage has already been paid. Respond as soon as possible. The sooner the better. Do not procrastinate and make appointments with borrowed time. The Lord is waiting to (re)introduce you to the vision of your life (identity) and the vision for your life (purpose).

e2I Living does not repurpose your life; it re-purposes your life! Embedding the beliefs and behaviors of *Imagination*, *Meditation*, *Contemplation*, *Irrigation*, *Celebration*, *Orientation*, and *Recalibration* into your daily living **does not repurpose you for a purpose other than the Lord's intended use**. Your life is not something "used for a different purpose to the one for which it was originally intended" (Cambridge English Dictionary). e2I Living (re)connects you to your original purpose for God's glory but (y)our good.

It beckons and equips you to do your first works over but with more:

- Clarity
- Conviction
- Commitment
- Grace
- Passion
- Gladness
- Precision and
- Presence

ESCHATOLOGY OF NOW

Eschatology is not merely 'the study of last things' related to a distant unknown (known) future. It is the doctrine of hope. A hope that not only confidently rests in a secured future; but a hope that revolutionizes and transforms the present. Faith develops into hope, causing not comfort but discomfort, not peace but disruption. Faith to live intentionally does not foster stillness in the heart but is itself this unsettled stillness in life.

Those who hope to rob the grave can no longer appease or give shelter to deferment, but begin to suffer under it, to undermine it. This kind of hope makes the lulled life a spent life. Hope that fuels constant disturbance to the settled notions of eventuality and counting time. ***It makes the beckoning invitation to a spent life the source of persistent new impulses***

towards the realization of an empty grave, where unused success refuses burial. Its days are spent making time count and seizing the day (see Ecclesiastes 3:12).

> THIS IS THE KIND OF DISCOMFORT THAT MANIFESTS WHEN A PERSON IS AWAKENED BY THE GOD OF LIFE AND TIME TO LIFE PURCHASED BY DEATH THAT EXPERIENCES RESURRECTION.

And more than this, this awakening is comforted by the blessed promise of transformation in the present and the unchangeable hope of resurrection in the future. **The "eschatology of now" revolutionizes, informs, and transforms the present.** Our loving God loves us intentionally. **He is just as concerned about our now as He is about then.**

DASH IT OUT

Life is short and with each passing day we are closer to the grave. Time is a gift. It is a present to your present. I salute you for not wanting to squander the time you have been given. Use it wisely and mark life.

> THE WORLD NEEDS TO KNOW YOU WERE HERE ONCE YOU HAVE GONE. LEAVE INFLUENCE AND IMPACT BEHIND, BUT DO NOT TAKE UNUSED SUCCESS WITH YOU.

I hope by reading *Moving at the Speed of Intention* that passion for purpose and living has been ignited in you. I hope a new level of determination has been awakened in you. Time is of the essence.

None of us know when our lives are going to expire. Hopefully reading this book has lit your resolve to give a benediction to procrastination. I pray it has given you the courage to detox from the addictive nature of eventuality. I hope it has emboldened and prepared you to snatch resignation, idleness, stagnation, and passive existence out of the grave and place them at the feet of Jesus.

The creative genius of God saw your life as necessary. Your existence is no accident. You were made for this! I hope reading this book helps you to honor the God of life by honoring Him in your life, with your life! God wants His glory to be on display and at work in it. Become a fulfilment of His faithfulness. **He intends for your redeemed and reimagined life to be "a mosaic of Jesus' beautiful face to the world"** (Gray, 2015, p. 311).

I hope by reading this book you feel more equipped to be found faithful with the currency God has entrusted to your capable care. I pray you feel more invigorated to eulogize 'saying yes' and 'doing no'. By the gift of His grace it is time to forever bury such cycles of sameness in (over) your life. The Father of time has given you time as a gift. So open it and open up to it! **Live intentionally and let God help you become an upgraded version of your best self.** Intention is waiting for you.

The God of the universe sent the invitation Himself. So, it should not surprise you that He has a vested interest in your success. ***You may be moving at the speed of intention, but things may not manifest at the rate you desire. Stay encouraged.*** Just know that heaven wants nothing more than for you to successfully settle your account with Jesus (see Matthew 25:19). Ask the Lord to add super to your natural!

A SUPERNATURAL AND REVOLUTIONARY EXISTENCE IS WAITING FOR YOU ON THE OTHER SIDE OF YES.

I hope by reading this book you have been provoked to ***give attention to intention***. Move swiftly with respect to time. With the Spirit's enablement, I pray it be used to forever disrupt any semblance of the status quo in your life. I hope reading it has awakened the giant in you and emboldened you to ***see and seize life through the eyes of the living God***. I pray this book compels you to take your goals, dreams, and desires off life support. I pray it ignites you to breathe new life into that spirit of procrastination → causing it to surrender its quick claim deed of your ambition, hopes, and aspirations.

I pray this book <u>lights a fire in your belly to journal</u> about your *'not yets'* or *'almosts'* or *'forgottens'* or *'abandoned'* or *'deferred'* or *'I can'ts'*. I pray reading it lovingly (boldly) confronts your idleness. I pray it radically breathes new life into areas of inactivity or unbelief in your life.

I hope this book beckons you to journal. I am in my prayer closet interceding; praying this work quickens a bold and sustainable affinity for action in you.

Pull ONE thing out of the grave! Identify ONE area of procrastination (<u>TO START WITH</u>)***.*** See it through the eyes of the living God. Actively partner with God to give it life and to nurture it. The Lord is yearning for you to become an e2I Champion! ***Pull ONE thing out of the procrastination casket*** and watch God create **patterns** and **pathways** to (*repeatable* and *sustainable*) success.

I pray reading this companion manuscript to the authoritative text of your religious tradition heightens your refusal to see yourself as a grasshopper. Christian Scripture teaches against such small thinking. Do not allow your fear to be magnified by what you perceive as giants. Do not craft or believe the exaggerated reports of what you may be up against. You are not insignificant, small, or weak. The grasshopper mentality is an enemy to your future. Remember the God factor!!

View your life through the lens of God's <u>unlimited</u> ***strength and resources. See yourself through the eyes of the living God***. Even when there is evidence of the obstacles, *view your Goliaths* (1 Samuel 17:4-7) and *Anaks* (Numbers 13:33) *through the eyes of the living God* (Joshua 2; 1 Sam. 17:24-26).

Silence the echoes (see Numbers 13:30), ***bring your thoughts captive*** (2 Corinthians 10:4-5; Proverbs 4:25-27), ***update your daily meal plan*** (Matthew 4:4; Psalm 42:1-2 and 63:1), ***elevate your mentality*** (Proverbs 23:7; Philippians 4:8), and ***push through the adversity to accomplish your God-sized dreams and God-shaped goals***. You are no grasshopper! You are a giant! Slay giants by actively partnering with God to pursue, practice, and possess God-shaped success (Philippians 1:6).

You are *acceptable* (Tit. 3:5-7), *chosen* (1 Pet. 2:9), *valuable* (Lk. 12:24), *lovable* (Jn. 3:16; Isa. 54:10), *capable* (Phil. 4:13; 2 Tim. 3:17), and the *apple of God's eye* (Ps. 17:8-9). YOU belong to God (1 Jn. 4:4; 1 Cor. 7:3). The power that lays within you and is at work for you is dynamite (2 Cor. 12:9)! And this power makes you dynamic (Eph. 3:20)!

E2I TRANSFORMATION IS READY TO IMPLODE INSIDE YOU

The gift of God's grace and power is yearning to change and charge the soul and substance of your life. They are also longing to transform the plight and flight of your life. The wait is over! Honor the creative, redemptive, and purposeful genius of God in your life. Let your new (or renewed) covenant and journey with intention begin, today! The intentional and transformative love of God is calling you. Fresh water is in your cup. New beginnings are chasing you down. Fresh wind is at your back.

- RECALIBRATED FAITH IS YOUR **GARMENT** (let it <u>wear</u> you).
- RESTORED PASSION IS YOUR **FUEL** (let it <u>inspire</u> and <u>nourish</u> you).
- REIMAGINED PURPOSE IS YOUR **INHERITANCE** (let it <u>possess</u> you).
- REPRIORITIZED LIVING IS YOUR **PRIZE** (let it <u>crown</u> you).

Because God-defined and God-honoring success is never individualistic, e2I transformation will rearrange lives and landscapes around you. Let your life be changed so you can embrace your identity as an infectious e2I champion (see **Appendix B**).

By reading this book, you have had the opportunity to learn:

- Intention has its own language and diet.
- The graveyard is pregnant with the offspring of eventuality and procrastination.
- God has called you to be a grave robber.
- You cannot rob the grave if you fail to RSVP to God's invitation to intentional living.
- God is responsible for success. You are responsible for faithfulness.
- Your future is auditioning in your present.
- Your present is auditioning for your future.
- You are the Master's masterpiece and magnum opus.
- God is longing for purpose and destiny to be released in you.
- Elevated thinking is required to elevate acting.

By reading this book, you have had the opportunity to learn:

- Your mindset and motives need to marinate so they can season your next season.
- Right environments and relationships stimulate, stretch, challenge, and upgrade you.
- Your destiny can and will be accelerated by the right mentoring, methods, and ministry.
- Detective definitions of success will deform and derail you.
- Wear your God-shaped dream so vision can wear you.
- Moving at the Speed of Intention is not only a lifestyle; it is an evolutionary and revolutionary existence.
- Seasons of bereavement should be spent conducting an inventory of what you gave rather than what you kept.
- The e2I tool suite equips you to live a spent life so you can depreciate the value of the most expensive real estate on the planet.

CONCLUSION

My big brothers (Tim and Darrell Johnson) are my heroes! #GoodStock. Their manhood remains a ministry to me. *To hear Darrell Anthony Johnson, Sr. repeatedly and passionately echo "live the dash" moves me to tears. It also provokes and intensifies my desire to live intentionally.* My brother's heart was understandably crushed on May 14, 2018. The life of his oldest prince D'Anthony Marcel Johnson, Sr. expired on that day… just days after his 26th birthday. And ever since May 24, 2018—the day D'Anthony was laid to rest—**"live the dash"** has been his loving father's clarion call. It arrests his communication (whether written or verbal... or in person or on social media). And it invigorates his life.

"Live the dash" is his anchor in that it is all he can hold on to at times. It comforts him. It ministers to him. ***Out of his own pain he encourages family and friends with this invitation from heaven.*** It has become joyful news to him. Akin to David's response to the Prophet Gad, "live the dash" is like Darrell is building an altar to God for this joyful news is beginning to turn his mourning into dancing (see Psalm 30:10-12).

This book is the eulogy I preached at my nephew's funeral. My sermon notes have been expanded to unpack and amplify the sentiments contained in his homily (see **Appendix C**). I pray *Moving at the Speed of Intention* contributes both to our healing and serves as a memorial in celebration of the life of D'Anthony Marcel Johnson, Sr. Like the urgency and courage of this young prince, it is time for you to recalibrate your gaze, refine your focus, reprioritize your life, and reenergize your passions. ***Let intention taxi to the runway of your life.***

My twin sister is hands down the smartest person I know. P. Diana Gray summarized the **e2I Model** and this work succinctly. May the **e2I Champion** in you feast sufficiently on this soul food's simplicity and significance before the balance of borrowed time in your life comes due. Three powerful words from my Wombmate: **"Dash It Out!"** *#iDash*

God has called you to be a grave robber. The LORD is longing for purpose and destiny to be released in you. This is the chief end of your existence. ***Glorify God and enjoy Him forever. Dash it out!*** *Moving at the Speed of Intention* is an evolutionary and revolutionary existence for at the end of your days an inventory will be conducted to determine what you gave rather than what you kept. ***The beliefs and behaviors in the e2I Tool Suite will equip you to rob the grave and turn tomorrow into today.***

Do not appease the grave; with God's enablement seek to undermine it. #DashitOut! Depreciate the value of the most expensive real estate on the planet. ***And refuse burial of unused success. The God of life and time is awakening you to a life purchased by the death of Christ that He has purposed to radically experience resurrection.*** Let the blessed hope of your secured future revolutionize and transform your present. Give a benediction to procrastination. End your illicit affair with eventuality.

From the dust we came and to the dust we will return (see Genesis 3:19). Let your dust give praise to God! ***Give praise by giving an account of the faithful use of the gifts of <u>life</u> and <u>time</u> the Lord has so graciously afforded you.*** Let your dust give praise to God when Christ comes to settle the account of your life. I pray your death is profitable and your dust gives praise to God and testifies of His faithfulness (see Psalm 30:9). #iDash. ***May intentional living declare Jesus' victory over the last enemy of creation – which is death.*** Selah. Christ died that you may live!! So make your time count and accept God's loving invitation to intentional living so you can LIVE! Let the *#e2IChampion* in you be unleashed so you can live a spent life for God's glory and for your good.

What are you going to pull out of the grave?!?! With the Spirit's enablement, actively partner with God and begin to ***pull gifts, dreams, ideas, and goals out of the procrastination casket. Watch the God of life give it life!*** Patterns and pathways to transformative and sustainable success await your RSVP. God has a vested interest in His definition of success for your life. Your dust is ready to praise God and testify of His faithfulness!

Tool Suite for Intentional Living

IMAGINATION
DREAMS • DESIRES • DECLARATIONS

CONTEMPLATION
ASPIRATION • PERSPIRATION

MEDITATION
SUPPLICATION • INTERCESSION

ANTICIPATION
CELEBRATION • SUCCESS

MANIFESTATION
ORIENTATION • RECALIBRATION

IRRIGATION
PLANT • REAP • HARVEST

e21

- Grant audience to your dreams (**IMAGINATION**)

- Pray for the will, way, wisdom, power, provision, and protection of God (**MEDITATION**)

- Give continued attention and focus to your God-sized and God-honoring recurring dreams, passions, and ideas (**CONTEMPLATION**)

- Water what's planted in you and what you're planting (**IRRIGATION**)

- Expect the expected and memorialize pause for applause moments (**ANTICIPATION & CELEBRATION**)

- Align your identity and goals with your preferred future (**ORIENTATION**)

- Optimize reflection and renewal to look back while moving forward (**RECALIBRATION**)

"Dash It Out!" Your future will thank you for it today! Your future is auditioning IN your present. Your present is auditioning FOR your future. *Move at the speed of intention. And turn tomorrow into today! Today!*

#Iame2I

Philippians 4:6-9 (New Living Translation)

⁶ Don't worry about anything; instead, pray about everything. Tell God what you need, and thank him for all He has done. ⁷ Then you will experience God's peace, which exceeds anything we can understand. His peace will guard your hearts and minds as you live in Christ Jesus. ⁸ And now, dear brothers and sisters, one final thing. **Fix your thoughts on what is true, and honorable, and right, and pure, and lovely, and admirable. Think about things that are excellent and worthy of praise.** ⁹ **Keep putting into practice all you learned and received from me** —everything you heard from me and saw me doing. Then the God of peace will be with you.

#iDig #iDash #iAme2I

APPENDIX A. NOTES FROM THE PIANO BENCH

Robert E. Webb, B.A., MTS
Living in the Key of Life (Discussion Points)

B NATURAL

1. No matter what key you start on, by following the pattern or at least familiarizing yourself with the pattern, you make transitioning to each new key an easy encounter.

2. **The problem for most piano students (and students of life) is they miss the lesson regarding the pattern.** Thus, they are relegated to fighting through searching for the proper position and visual clues required by the new key signature with only their ear serving as judge.

3. Chords, like the scale are also based on patterns. C Major Chord = C + E + G (Root [or 1], up four [4] keys then up three [3] more keys). *No matter how it's voiced (ordered or spelled), it's still a C Major Chord.*
   - C Major Chord (Root Position) = C + E + G (1 + 4 + 3)
   - C Major Chord (First Inversion) = E + G + C (1 + 3 + 5)
   - C Major Chord (Second Inversion) = G + C + E (1 + 5 + 4)

The same pattern can be applied to any other key. **The same is true with most situations in life: once the pattern of behavior is identified, then appropriate action can be taken for the best possible result.**

4. **Just as it is in life, we cannot always live life on a Major Chord.** We will sometimes encounter accidentals that will alter our perception of where we are (turning that major chord into a minor chord). Minor chords in Western musicology are generally associated with sadness, anger or other negative feelings.
   - **Minor is not failure unless that's is what you intended!**
   - **Minor can also be success if that's what you intend!**

5. Many of us consider one *minor* setback enough to make an otherwise perfect life a *major* failure. One must consider that musically speaking,

any organized movement or harmonic succession of chords **is called a** *progression*.
- **Moving from a minor chord to a major chord is a progression.**
- **But moving from a major chord to a minor chord is not a regression.**
- Moving from a major chord to a minor chord is still a progression.

Progression defined is "the process of developing or moving gradually **towards a more advanced state**" according to Oxford Dictionaries. Hence the idea of *"falling* [or *failing*] *forward*

6. Consider one of the most well-known songs in the wedding repertoire: ***Pachelbel's Canon in D***. The progression pattern is simple yet pointed: Major, major, *minor, minor*, major, major, major, major. Even with the two consecutive *minor* chords, it's still a beautifully calming masterpiece.
   - **There may be success after success, but one cannot become discouraged when experiencing failure after failure.**
   - **Remember the pattern, although painful, is still progression.**

You are still moving toward the end of your own personal *magnum opus*. **Each measure is created by the decisions and responses and/or reactions that you make.** The question is **what are your intending the melody to be?"**

7. Failure is not failure unless that is what you intended. Consider the orchestral piece ***"Unanswered Question" by Charles Ives***. The perennial question of existence is posed in the beginning; however, where one would expect a final resolution and response to the question, the listener is met with still another more intriguing question. **This is a literary tool employed even by the writer of the Book of Jonah, which ends with a question**: "And should not I spare Nineveh, that great city, wherein are more than six-score thousand persons that cannot discern between their right hand and their left hand; and also much cattle?" (Jonah 4:11, KJV).

APPENDIX B. e2I TRAITS

Patrick J. Oliver, Ph.D., D.Min.
Behaviors of an e2I Champion

Chapter 1: Eventuality vs. Intentionality

- ❖ e2I champions realize that empty dreams, unmet goals, and abandoned plans are still waiting to materialize in their lives.
- ❖ e2I champions realize the frustrated cargo circling their address is waiting for them to approve delivery. They know the manifest is longing for their signature so it can manifest in their lives.
- ❖ e2I champions understand the wait has waited on them long enough.
- ❖ e2I champions are committed to amending any agendas that keep them from the itinerary of their future.
- ❖ e2I champions are passionate about giving a benediction to procrastination. They desire to end their barren and illicit affair with eventuality.
- ❖ e2I champions know that their future will thank them for it today!

Chapter 2: Your Move (First Steps)

- ❖ e2I champions embrace the revelation that living intentionally has taxied to the runway of their lives.
- ❖ e2I champions realize intentionality has already experienced lift off.
- ❖ e2I champions are willing to let intentional living gain elevation and soar.
- ❖ e2I champions know that mistakes, false starts, disappointments, and frustrations are part of life. However, they know such seasons are not meant to be destinations.
- ❖ e2I champions are passionate about trusting God to turn their mourning into dancing.
- ❖ e2I champions refuse to let violations imprison their victory.

- ❖ e2I champions are willing to be deliberate about not making appointments with borrowed time.
- ❖ e2I champions want to get out of 'the could' and into 'the should'.

Chapter 3: Cancelled Reservations

- ❖ e2I champions are driven to take the microphone from *'would of / could of / should of'* because they have testified enough on their behalf.
- ❖ e2I champions believe immobility, inactivity, & idleness have run their course. They realize it is time to run a new course.
- ❖ e2I champions are committed to be shaken from resignation and from sleep walking through life.
- ❖ e2I champions are passionate about living full and dying empty.
- ❖ e2I champions are committed to robbing the grave!

Chapter 4: RSVP to God's Invitation

- ❖ e2I champions believe that time is precious and perishable.
- ❖ e2I champions want to make the best possible use of their allotted time.
- ❖ e2I champions realize the importance of healthy environments and relationships.
- ❖ e2I champions look for healthy relationships to stretch them. They also hunger for God-honoring environments to provide clarity, context, and currency for their present.
- ❖ e2I champions are committed to building and honoring relationships that function as a lifeline to their future.
- ❖ e2I champions believe healthy atmospheres and relationships dares them to be great.
- ❖ e2I champions are heaven-bent on having the God-shaped greatness in them be encouraged and equipped to the glory of God.

Chapter 5: Inhale Purpose. Exhale Destiny.

- ❖ e2I champions are burdened with the thought that the most expensive real estate on the planet is the cemetery.
- ❖ e2I champions realize the graveyard is pregnant with unused success and treasures that make God weep.
- ❖ e2I champions are passionate about ministering to the heart of God by inhaling purpose and exhaling destiny.
- ❖ e2I champions realize it takes dependence on God to trust His wisdom and direction to identify and resurrect their gifts, highlighting where they intersect with their passions.

Chapter 6: Living in the Key of Life: B Natural

- ❖ e2I champions are willing to read the fine print of God's invitation to intentional living and rely on the gift of God's grace and power to use their injuries, examine their blind spots, and reject being resistant to mirrors.
- ❖ e2I champions are committed to trusting the Master Composer to help them master the accidental notes in their lives for His glory and for their good.
- ❖ e2I champions embrace the rhythm of their lives. They realize there is harmony to their lives, in their lives, and for their lives.
- ❖ e2I champions realize they are direct benefactors of divine endowment and provision.
- ❖ e2I champions believe that God knows the key signature He has ordained for their lives. They realize it takes dependence on the Spirit to live in the key of life.

Chapter 7: The Testimony of Tattoos

- ❖ e2I champions know that intentional living brands God's Name and face on their lives.
- ❖ e2I champions realize God's answer to humanity's longing for purpose, direction, and significance is manifested when they accept His invitation to intentional living. They are courageous pioneers who know the signature of God will not show up in invisible ink in their lives. Rather, it will display His manifold wisdom to showcase the love of Christ to draw and inspire others through their testimony.

- e2I champions rely on the gift of God's grace and power to work in and through them to live God-honoring spent lives.

Chapter 8: Conversations with the Pregnant Graveyard

- e2I champions begin with the end in mind.
- e2I champions refuse to be exempt from living because they realize they are not exempt refuse from dying.
- e2I champions to let 'not yet' cripple them. They recognize that sometimes being too scared to dream can make resignation feel safe.
- e2I champions realize it takes reliance on the Spirit to forge a new future, be drawn nearer to God's heart, and be equipped to courageously implement strategies to counteract the 'nevers of life' from being swallowed up.
- e2I champions believe that God does not want any of the stuff back He has deposited in them. They reject the status quo and are heaven-bent on not burying the currency God has invested in them.

Chapter 9: Turn Tomorrow into Today

- e2I champions realize that the speed of intention is connected to purposeful activity.
- e2I champions are committed to valuing incremental steps.
- e2I champions move beyond the sunken place and re-cast their thoughts to other roles in the production of their lives.
- e2I champions refuse to allow what they are not doing to hijack their gaze. They look for ways to grant sufficient audience to what they are doing.
- e2I champions are passionate about actively partnering with God in their preferred future.
- e2I champions rely on the gift of God's grace and power to turn their tomorrow into today.

Chapter 10: LivINg the Dream

- ❖ e2I champions are passionate about moving beyond the well-established cultural norms that are infected with commercialism, consumerism, and capitalism. They reject defective definitions of success and are committed to redefining success from God's eternal perspective.
- ❖ e2I champions know that moving at the speed of intention gives life and lift to their dreams.
- ❖ e2I champions realize God's divine fingerprint is constantly on display. They believe delayed manifestation is often a dress rehearsal for the tailored plan God has tailored just for them.

Chapter 11: Tolls on the Road to Intention

- ❖ e2I champions realize there are costs on the journey of intention.
- ❖ e2I champions are committed to learning about the necessary and approved currency on the journey of intention. They embrace the call for readiness and want to be better equipped in the stewardship of it.
- ❖ e2I champions are burdened with the thought that without the power of God's presence, peace, and love, the numbing and addictive deceptions of procrastination will intensify in the lives of people.
- ❖ e2I champions believe that from dust we came and dust we will return. They are passionate about letting their dust give praise to God.

Chapter 12: e2I (eventual to Intentional)

- ❖ e2I champions refuse to believe that they can live their best lives divorced from the counsel and purposes of God.
- ❖ e2I champions count the cost but move forward anyway, knowing that God's grace is sufficient to empower them to fulfill the task of reaping the interest of heaven on earth.
- ❖ e2I champions welcome the blessed burden to make every day a gift rather than a coffin. They know this will cost them relationships with convenience, complacency, and resignation, along with systems and environments, who traffic in procrastination and accommodation.
- ❖ e2I champions are passionate about living a God-pleasing spent life.
- ❖ e2I champions are driven by beliefs and behaviors that emboldens and equips them to live the dash, rob the grave, and turn tomorrow into today to the glory of God.
- ❖ e2I champions believe intentional living declares Jesus' victory over the last enemy of creation – which is death.
#iDig #iDash #iAme2I

APPENDIX C. EULOGY SERMON NOTES

Scripture – Psalm 90:12
Title – "Living the Dash: Accepting the Invitation to Intention"

There is powerful symbol that will brand and mark each of our lives… it will be attached to all of us. It will stain all our epitaphs and score the inscriptions of our graves. This brand, this mark, this stain, this powerful symbol is **THE DASH**.
- The dash between sunrise and sunset echoes an authentic and inclusive sentiment.
- It contains either a thunderous testimony or a whimpering whisper; nonetheless it will speak.

The dash does not merely testify of how long we have lived, but how we have lived. Charles A. Tidwell, past Distinguished Professor of Administration and Chair of Denominational Relationships at Southwestern Baptist Theological Seminary said, "**Quality makes quantity meaningful**". So, the dash is not silent! It speaks… in it is a testimony of how long we have lived but more importantly it speaks of how we have lived. In Psalms 30:9 David asked God *"what profit is there in my death… will the dust praise You? Will it tell of Your faithfulness?"*
- **TATOO:** we may or may not like tats… **D'Anthony's 1st tattoo… mamma's face & name on it** (**Point** – the dash will stain, brand, and mark all our lives; how will God's face and name be on the dash?)

Death has a way of making all of us captive audiences as it confronts our finite existence, exposes our frailty, and reminds us of our humanity. These realities also invite us to **stop counting time** and should subsequently quicken us to **start making time count**. God created time when He created the universe. **Time**… the indefinite progress of existence measured in seconds, hours, minutes, moments, days, weeks, months, and years was God's invention to keep everything from happening at once. God created time as a limited part of His creation for accommodating the workings of His purpose.

With each new dawn, we have one day less to live; we are one day nearer the grave. **Time is precious!**

- In Ps. 39:4, 5 David said – *"You have made my days a mere handbreadth; the span of my years is as nothing before you. Each man's life is but a breath"*
- In the conclusion of the book of James the Apostle challenges us not to boast about tomorrow.
  - *[13] Come now, you who say, "Today or tomorrow we will go into such and such a town and spend a year there and trade and make a profit"* (James 4:13, 14)
  - *[14] yet you do not know what tomorrow will bring.* **What is your life?** *For you are a mist* **that appears for a little time and then vanishes.**
  - *[15] Instead you ought to say, "If the Lord wills, we will live and do this or that."*
- In Ephesians 5:15, 16 the Apostle Paul exhorts us "Be very careful, then, **how you live**—not as unwise but as wise, **making the most of every opportunity**, because the days are evil"

- Time is not only precious! It is also perishable! It is a non-renewable commodity and perishable resource that God invites us to use intentionally.
- While it may sound quaint or familiar, lacking the urgency of now... we should not take the precious resource of time for granted.
- While it may even sound religious or rehearsed, disincentivizing the truth... we are indeed **living on borrowed time**. To live as God would have us live, it is essential we make the best possible use of our allotted time.

<u>When will we stop:</u>
(a) divorcing our individual and collective consciousness from the beckoning gift of the present (b) robing our frail humanity in disarming, comfortable, complacent, and even arrogant denial
(c) rejecting God's loving and lifting, patient yet persistent invitation to live intentionally and with intentionality
(d) passively and ignorantly refusing to live life on purpose and with purpose?

When will we accept that we are indeed living on time that has both been (1) borrowed from the Father of it and (2) gifted to us?

Dr. Myles Munroe was right… **the most expensive real estate on the planet is not the diamond mines of South Africa or the oil fields of Iran or Iraq or Kuwait or the uranium mines of the Soviet Union.** The most expensive real estate in the world is not properties in Florida, France, Dubai, London, New York, Belgium, or India ranging from $35M - $1B (according to 2018 market values).

The most expensive and wealthiest place in the world are not gold mines or oil fields or diamond mines or banks. **The most expensive real estate on the planet is the cemetery, the graveyard.**

- Companies never started // Books never written // Masterpieces never painted // Words never spoken
- Dreams that were never fulfilled // ideas that never became reality // visions that were never manifested, songs that were never written // decisions never made // potential never released
- The cemetery is pregnant with unused success… buried in the cemetery are treasures that make God weep

In Psalms 90 Moses focuses on **God's greatness, our human weakness**, and **our need for the Lord to provide grace for our daily needs**. We are to seek wisdom and to live each day to its fullest for the glory of God.

The Book of Psalms is the hymn book of Israel. Most biblical scholars believe that Moses wrote Psalms 90 as a prayer for God's mercy during the 40 years of Israel's wandering in the wilderness. Moses was in the wilderness with the Children of Israel at the time of this writing.

Let's look at our text and glean life lessons as we overhear the prayer of Moses in what is considered the oldest psalms:
1. In verses 1&2, Moses emphasizes & declares the eternal nature of God; from everlasting to everlasting You are God.
- God was the dwelling place despite their sorrow and oppression
- In vv 3-6, Moses speaks of the fragile nature of humanity… c.f. v3; the brevity of human life… we are formed from the dust and from the dust we must return;
- In vv 5 & 6; Moses testifies that life is so temporary! Our time on earth is short.
- Life is like grass, which, though changing under the influence of the night's dew, and flourishing in the morning, is soon cut down and withers.

- So, we see Man's Frailty against the backdrop of God's Eternity

HERE IS THE SHOUT IN THE TEXT!!!! In vv7-8, Moses highlights humanity's sinful nature & our shortcomings before God… c.f. v8, our iniquities are set before God; our secret sins are placed in the light of His presence.
- Every deed, every word, every inmost thought is open to the One who dwells in eternity and there's no fleeing from His loving presence

2. In vv9-11, Moses stresses how short life is in comparison to the eternal nature of God → Time is borrowed

3. In v12, Moses implores us not to literally count each day but to make each day count… Moses literally says, "since I am bound by time may God teach me how to number my days so I might use my time wisely."

✓ A good way to gain wisdom is to learn to live each day with an eternal perspective.
✓ C. S. Lewis understood this: **"If you read history you will find that the Christians who did the most for the present world were just those who thought most of the next."**
✓ Let our activities be governed by the consciousness of eternity.

Like D'Anthony Marcel Johnson, Sr., we need to be conscious of our limited time and plan the eternal into our lives. D'Anthony was an encourager and a champion of life… he was sold out to the success of other people.

4. V17 → Let the beauty of the Lord be seen in you

Even during his own wilderness experience, Moses prays that the favor and beauty of God… that His gracious acts, in their harmony, be illustrated in us, and favor our enterprise.

And by extension, one could make the argument that Moses—after beseeching the Lord to teach us to number our days… to teach us not to count time but to make time count… to teach us to desire life not to show up in invisible ink but rather to humbly & intentionally desire to mark the pages of His-story—one could rightly surmise that the high watermark and heartbeat of Moses' prayer is for each generation to be sold out to **Disappointing the Cemetery**… to robbing the graveyard of your treasures (**untapped power, dormant strength,**

all you can be but you haven't become yet); to intentionally depreciate the value of the most expensive real estate on the planet… to rob the grave of the dreams that you still carry on the inside of you → to disappoint the cemetery of unfilled purpose, untapped potential, and unreleased possibility.

On May 21, 2018 @ 2:03pm (getting on the Walzem ramp on 410S); Darrell Anthony Johnson, Sr. said…
- "If I was there with him, I would have jumped in front of the bullet to take it for him so he could still be here." **Sounds like Calvary in miniature!!**
- "Through D'Anthony's death, his son lives on."

References

Barnes, A. (1980). *Barnes' notes on the old & new testaments: 27 volumes, an explanatory and practical commentary.* Baker House Publishing: Grand Rapids, MI.

Bradford, C. (2016, February 07). Tough to a fault: Bam Morris' wild story 20 years after Super Bowl XXX. Retrieved from https://www.timesonline.com/article/20160206/sports/302069997

Cole, E. L. (1982). *Maximized Manhood.* Whitaker House: New Kensington, PA.

Conley, S. J. (2017). Lead with love. Digi-Tall Media: Dallas, TX.

Crank, N. (2017). *Hi God (It's Me Again): What to Pray When You Don't Know What to Say.* Fedd Books: Austin, TX.

Foster, Chiffon R. (2018). *Destiny Decoded.* Level Up Media: Dallas, TX.

GotQuestions.org. (2009, May 17). What does the Bible say about how to find purpose in life? Retrieved from https://www.gotquestions.org/purpose-of-life.html

Gray, D. L. (2015). *The high definition leader: Building multiethnic churches in a multiethnic world.* Thomas Nelson Publishers: Nashville, TN.

King Jr., Martin. L. (1963). *Strength to Love.* Harper & Row: New York, NY.

King, M. L., Jr. (1963, September 18). Eulogy for the Martyred Children. Retrieved from https://kinginstitute.stanford.edu/king-papers/documents/eulogy-martyred-children

Lewis, C.S. (1952). Mere Christianity. HarperOne Publishers: New York, NY.

Montgomery, J. W. (1969). *Ecumenicity, Evangelicals, and Rome.* Zondervan Publishing House: Grand Rapids, MI.

Munroe, M. (1991). *Understanding your potential: Discovering the hidden you.* Destiny Image Publishers: Shippensburg, PA.

Nichols, S. J. (2013). *Bonhoeffer on the Christian Life: From the Cross, for the World*. Wheaton: Crossway, 2013.

Piper, J. (1983, August 21). Do not grow weary in well-doing. Retrieved from https://www.desiringgod.org/messages/do-not-grow-weary-in-well-doing

Stott, J. R. (2006). The cross of Christ. InterVarsity Press: Westmont, IL.

The Dash (2019). The Dash a Poem by Linda Ellis. Retrieved from https://thedashpoem.com/

Thomas, Frank. (2017, September 4). **A Conversation with Rev. Dr. Claudette Anderson Copeland hosted by Dr. Frank A. Thomas**. Retrieved from https://www.youtube.com/watch?v=rHToFCfolEY

Tidwell, C. A. (1985). *Church administration: Effective leadership for ministry*. B&H Academic: Nashville, TN.

Vanderklay, P. (2006, October). Tim Keller's use of identity in his theology. Retrieved from https://paulvanderklay.me/2009/10/26/tim-kellers-use-of-identity-in-his-theology/.

Werpehowski, W. (2007). Practical wisdom and the integrity of Christian life. *Journal of the Society of Christian Ethics, 27*(2), 55-72.

Wilmington, H.L. (1981). *Wilmington's guide to the Bible*. Tyndale House Publishers: Carol Stream, IL.

About the Author

Patrick Oliver is the President and CEO of Loving YOU to Life (LYTL) Ministries in Dallas, Texas. LYTL exists to love, lift, and lead organizations and persons to inherit, disciple, and steward their God-shaped and God-sized success. A United States Air Force veteran, he has served in military chapel support ministry around the world and as Chief Servant / Lead Pastor of churches in the Pacific Northwest and the Midwest. Due to his continued attention to intention, he has earned a Doctor in Ministry and a Ph.D. in Organizational Leadership. He considers mentoring critical currency to living a spent life. Dr. P. received leadership training at Harvard, Cornell, Notre Dame, and Seattle Universities in his pursuit to be more hero maker than hero. He has a passion for promoting unity in diversity in response to the multiethnic mosaic constructed in the mind of our intentional God. Always confronting and challenging distorted definitions of success, Patrick is a champion of viewing and experiencing victorious living through the eyes of God.

Write an Amazon Book Review:

Please take the time write a book review even if you did not purchase "Moving at the Speed of Intention" off Amazon. If you find anything valuable or enlightening in the book I encourage you to post it on Amazon!! Your review may really help other readers, which is why I wrote the book. Let's build an e2I Community together. Our futures will thank us for it today! Become an e2I Champion and share your thoughts with others.

To contact the Author:

Dr. Patrick J. Oliver
www.drpatrickjoliver.com
drpwjoliver@att.net
(877) 782-9068

NOTE: no work is ever perfect. Edits to this manuscript were made on June 10, 2019.

Made in the USA
Columbia, SC
24 June 2019